How to Heal

In the depth of winter,
I finally learned that within me
there lay an invincible summer.

ALBERT CAMUS

How to Heal Depression

Dr Harold H. Bloomfield
& Peter McWilliams

Thorsons
An Imprint of HarperCollinsPublishers

Thorsons
An Imprint of HarperCollins*Publishers*
77–85 Fulham Palace Road,
Hammersmith, London W6 8JB

First published by Prelude Press 1983
8159 Santa Monica Boulevard
Los Angeles, California 90046

Published by Thorsons 1995
3 5 7 9 10 8 6 4

Harold H. Bloomfield, M.D. and Peter McWilliams
assert the moral right to
be identified as the authors of this work

A catalogue record for this book
is available from the British Library

ISBN 0 7225 3135 4

Printed and bound in Great Britain by
Caledonian International Book Manufacturing Ltd, Glasgow

Nothing in this book is intended to constitute medical
advice, treatment or specific prescription. Medical
diagnosis can only occur between an individual patient
and his or her physician.

I contemplated suicide.
My main concern was that
I would not make
the <u>New</u> <u>York</u> <u>Times</u>
obituary page.

ART BUCHWALD

DEDICATION

To my wonderful wife Sirah,
who loved me through
my healing process.

—Harold H. Bloomfield

For Melba and Harold,
who helped me out
of depression.
Thank you.

—Peter McWilliams

*No one is as capable of gratitude
as one who has emerged
from the kingdom of night.*

ELIE WIESEL

*During depression
the world disappears.
Language itself.
One has nothing to say.
Nothing.*

KATE MILLET

Authors' Notes

Welcome.

Our goal is to make this book brief, practical, and to-the-point.

The *last* thing a person with depression wants is an intricate tome, heavy with footnotes, citations, Latin words, and sentences such as "Depression is a biopsychosocial disorder, sometimes treated with monoamine oxidase inhibitors."

We have also included quotes from people, some well known and some not, across many cultures and centuries, to show that depression—and the desire to heal it—is a deeply human and universal experience.

Our approach to the treatment of depression is twofold. Each part is equally important.

- One is healing the brain, as current medical research points to biochemical imbalances in the brain as the seat of depression.

- The other is healing the mind—overcoming negative habits of thought and action which may cause, or be caused by, depression.

Treating the brain *and* the mind is the most effective way to heal depression. Recent medical and psychological breakthroughs make depression among the most successfully treatable of all serious illnesses.

Harold H. Bloomfield, M.D.
Peter McWilliams

Del Mar, California
February 20, 1994

I am in that temper
that if I were under water
I would scarcely kick
to come to the top.

KEATS

About This Book

Our book is divided into four parts.

In Part I, **"Understanding Depression,"** we discuss what depression is (and is not); how you can be depressed without "feeling depressed"; and the possible causes and ramifications of depression. There's even a short self-evaluation for depression, compliments of the National Institutes of Health (page 22).

In Part II, **"Healing the Brain,"** we look at the biological causes of depression and, more importantly, its medical treatment. This includes antidepressant medication, nutrition, exercise and such strenuous activities as hot baths and massage. This is the domain of the psychiatrist, family doctor, and other healthcare specialists.

Part III we call **"Healing the Mind."** We explore unlearning mental habits either caused by or contributing to depression, while learning new mental patterns that tend to enhance effectiveness, well-being, and emotional freedom. We discuss exciting new short-term therapies (usually only ten to twenty sessions) that have proven to be highly successful in healing depression. This is the domain of the psychologist, psychiatrist, clinical social worker, and mental health professional.

The final section, Part IV, is **"As Healing Continues . . . ."** Although most people treated for depression find remarkable results within a short time, the complete healing of depression often continues for a while. There are ups and downs, lessons to be learned, new pathways to be explored.

Thank you for joining us on this healing journey.

CONTENTS

UNDERSTANDING DEPRESSION

HEALING THE BRAIN

HEALING THE MIND

AS HEALING CONTINUES . . .

*As a confirmed melancholic,
I can testify that the best
and maybe the only antidote
for melancholia is action.
However, like most melancholics,
I suffer also from sloth.*

EDWARD ABBEY

How to
Heal
Depression

I have heard that in ancient times
human beings lived
to the age of a hundred.
In our time,
we are exhausted
at the age of fifty.
Is this because of
changes in the circumstances,
or is it the fault of men?

SU WEN
4500 B.C.

Part I

Understanding Depression

In this part, we answer the basic questions about depression: What is depression? What causes it? How does one get it? How is it healed?

One:
You Are Not Alone

- If you or someone you know is depressed, you are not alone.

- *That's* something of an understatement.

- One in twenty Americans currently suffers from a depression severe enough to require medical treatment.

- One person in five will have a depression at some time in his or her life.

- Depression in its various forms (insomnia, fatigue, anxiety, stress, vague aches and pains, etc.) is the most common complaint heard in doctors' offices.

- Two percent of all children and five percent of all adolescents suffer from depression.

- More than twice as many women are currently being treated for depression than men. (It is not known whether this is because women are more likely to be depressed, or whether men tend to deny their depression.)

- People over sixty-five are four times more likely to suffer depression than the rest of the population.

- Depression is the #1 public health problem in this country. Depression is an epidemic—an epidemic on the rise.

I am now experiencing myself
all the things that
as a third party
I have witnessed going on
in my patients—
days when I slink about
depressed.

SIGMUND FREUD

Two:
If You Need It,
Get Help at Once

- If you think you need help, don't hesitate. Get it at once. Call your doctor.

- If you feel suicidal and are afraid you might act on it, please call 999, your doctor, a crisis prevention hotline, or go immediately to your local hospital emergency room. (Our thoughts on suicide are on page 36.)

- You should also seek help at once if you . . .

    —feel you are "coming apart"
    —are no longer in control
    —are about to take an action you may later regret
    —turn to alcohol, drugs, or other addictive substances in time of need
    —feel isolated with no one to turn to

- This is no time to "be brave" and attempt to "go it alone." In fact, asking for help takes enormous courage.

I was much further out
than you thought
And not waving but drowning.

S TEVIE S MITH

Three:
There Is No Need to Suffer

- More than eighty percent of the people with depression can be successfully treated.

- Long-term, expensive treatments are seldom necessary.

- Modern treatment for most depression is anti-depressant medication and short-term "talk" therapy—usually just ten to twenty sessions.

- Treatment for depression is relatively inexpensive—but whatever the cost, it is more than made up for in increased productivity, efficiency, physical health, improved relationships, and enjoyment of life.

- Yes, life will always have its "slings and arrows of outrageous fortune," and, yes, they will hurt. But there's no need to suffer from depression as well.

Pain is inevitable.
Suffering is optional.

M. KATHLEEN CASEY

Four:
"I Can't Handle Anything Else!"

- One of the most common feelings people with depression have is, "Enough!" "I've had it!" "I can't take any more."

- When we discuss treatment for depression, it may sound as if we're asking you to add yet another ton or two to your already overburdened life. Although it may *seem* this way, effective treatment for depression will *lighten* your load.

- Yes, we are asking you to visit "healthcare professionals," and, yes, a simple suggestion such as "Find a doctor or psychiatrist who specializes in the treatment of depression" can seem awfully intimidating.

- *But it will be worth it.*

- Most people respond to treatment for depression swiftly—usually in a matter of weeks. You may not feel "better than good" overnight, but the sense of being overburdened, overworked, and overwhelmed should significantly ease in a short time.

- Treatment for depression doesn't *take* time, it *makes* time.

I am now the most
miserable man living.
If what I feel
were equally distributed
to the whole human family,
there would be not one
cheerful face on earth.
Whether I shall ever be better,
I cannot tell.
I awfully forebode I shall not.
To remain as I am is impossible.
I must die or be better
it appears to me.

ABRAHAM LINCOLN

WHO SUFFERED
FROM DEPRESSION
MOST OF HIS ADULT LIFE

Five:
"Why Bother?"

- Another common symptom of depression, as voiced by Hamlet: "How weary, stale, flat, and unprofitable seem to me all the uses of this world!"

- Questions such as "Who cares?" "What's the point?" and "Why bother?" circulate in the mind of the depressed person.

- Unfortunately, this *symptom* of depression can keep one from seeking treatment. It becomes a vicious cycle: as the untreated depression worsens, the person feels that life is less and less worthwhile. As the person feels that life is less and less worthwhile, he or she is less likely to seek treatment.

- Depression is an illness that robs one of the meaning of life. Heal the illness. Enthusiasm, well-being, and a sense of life's purpose will return.

*It is the feeling
that nothing is worth while
that makes men ill
and unhappy.*

DR. HAROLD W. DODDS

Six:
It's Not Your Fault

- You didn't *do* anything to become depressed.

- Your *failure* to do something didn't cause your depression.

- Depression is an *illness*.

- You are no more at fault for having depression than if you had asthma, diabetes, heart disease, or any other illness.

- In becoming depressed, you have nothing to blame yourself for and nothing to feel guilty about. (Although two of the symptoms of depression are that you probably *will* blame yourself and you probably *will* feel guilty.)

- A predisposition toward depression can be hereditary. In addition, life is full of bumps and potholes—many of which simply cannot be avoided. It's not surprising, then, if one of them (or a collection of them) triggers a depressive illness.

- So, for heaven's sake, don't blame yourself. Don't even blame yourself for blaming yourself.

- It's not your fault.

*Guilt is the
mafia of the mind.*

BOB MANDEL

Seven:
It's Not _Anybody's_ Fault

- It's not your parents' fault. (If your depression is genetically based, your parents got it from their parents; their parents got it from their parents. How far back can blame go?)

- It's not your spouse or lover's fault.

- It's not your children's fault.

- It's not your boss's fault.

- It's not society's fault.

- It's not God's fault.

- No one is to blame.

- One of the symptoms of depression is feeling victimized—"They're doing it to me." Many people seem more willing to admit that they're _oppressed_ rather than _depressed_.

- Depression is simply an illness you somehow got—like low thyroid—which, while serious, is easily treated. The chances for complete recovery are excellent.

- _Where_ your depression came from isn't important; how to heal it is.

*I grew up to have
my father's looks,
my father's speech patterns,
my father's posture,
my father's opinions,
and my mother's
contempt for my father.*

JULES FEIFFER

Eight:
What Is Depression?

- We will do our best not to overburden you with technical terms and healthcare jargon. A few terms, however, are important to know.

- First, the word *depression* itself. In this book, when we speak of depression, we are speaking of what is medically known as *clinical depression*. We're discussing a specific illness that requires clinical intervention—hence *clinical* depression.

- We are not discussing the pain that immediately follows loss, or the "down" cycle in life's ordinary ups and downs.

- Nor are we discussing the popular use of the word *depressed*, which usually means *disappointed*. ("The coffee machine ran out. I'm depressed.")

- When we use *depression*, we're talking about a specific medical illness—one with a highly effective treatment.

*The term clinical depression
finds its way into too many
conversations these days.
One has a sense that
a catastrophe has occurred
in the psychic landscape.*

LEONARD COHEN

Nine:
The Three Primary Types
of Depression

- There are three primary forms of depression.

    —*Major Depression.* Like the flu, major depression has a beginning, a middle, and an end. Unlike the flu, major depressions often last for months. Left untreated, they tend to reoccur. Each reoccurrence tends to last longer and is more debilitating than the one before.

    —*Chronic Depression.* Chronic depression is a low-grade, long-term depression that can go on for years. Some people have had it most of their lives. Long-term, low-grade depression is also known as *dysthymia*—*dys*, meaning disorder, and *thymia* for mood. Dysthymia, then, is a disorder of one's mood.

    —*Manic-Depression.* Here the lows of depression can alternate with days or weeks of *mania*—extreme elation, unreasonably grandiose thoughts, and inappropriate, sometimes destructive actions. This is also known as *bipolar* depression, because the manic-depressive person fluctuates from one emotional pole (down) to the opposite pole (up) in unpredictable, rapid swings. (By contrast, major depression is unipolar—it focuses on only one pole: down.)

- We'll discuss other types of depression later. For now, let's take a look at that burning question, "Am I depressed?"

The aggravated agony
of depression
is terrifying,
and elation,
its nonidentical twin sister,
is even more terrifying—
attractive as she may be
for a moment.
You are grandiose
beyond the reality
of your creativity.

JOSHUA LOGAN

WHO SUFFERED FROM
MANIC-DEPRESSION

Ten:
The Symptoms of Depression

After careful evaluation, the National Institutes of Health developed the following checklist:

Symptoms of Depression Can Include
- ☐ Persistent sad or "empty" mood
- ☐ Loss of interest or pleasure in ordinary activities, including sex
- ☐ Decreased energy, fatigue, being "slowed down"
- ☐ Sleep disturbances (insomnia, early-morning waking, or oversleeping)
- ☐ Eating disturbances (loss of appetite and weight, or weight gain)
- ☐ Difficulty concentrating, remembering, making decisions
- ☐ Feelings of guilt, worthlessness, helplessness
- ☐ Thoughts of death or suicide, suicide attempts
- ☐ Irritability
- ☐ Excessive crying
- ☐ Chronic aches and pains that don't respond to treatment

In the Workplace, Symptoms of Depression Often May Be Recognized by
- ☐ Decreased productivity
- ☐ Morale problems
- ☐ Lack of cooperation
- ☐ Safety problems, accidents
- ☐ Absenteeism
- ☐ Frequent complaints of being tired all the time
- ☐ Complaints of unexplained aches and pains
- ☐ Alcohol and drug abuse

Symptoms of Mania Can Include
- ☐ Excessively "high" mood
- ☐ Irritability
- ☐ Decreased need for sleep
- ☐ Increased energy and activity
- ☐ Increased talking, moving, and sexual activity
- ☐ Racing thoughts
- ☐ Disturbed ability to make decisions
- ☐ Grandiose notions
- ☐ Being easily distracted

Eleven:
Are You Depressed?

- *"A thorough diagnosis is needed if four or more of the symptoms of depression or mania persist for more than two weeks,"* says the National Institutes of Health, *"or are interfering with work or family life."*

- The symptoms on the facing page are *not* "just life." If four or more of the symptoms have been a regular part of your life for more than two weeks or tend to interfere with your life in a regular way, a consultation with a physician experienced in diagnosing and treating depression is in order.

- You need not suffer any longer. Treatment is readily available.

- *"With available treatment, eighty percent of the people with serious depression—even those with the most severe forms—can improve significantly,"* says the National Institutes of Health. *"Symptoms can be relieved, usually in a matter of weeks."*

- Please talk to your doctor. (And read on!)

Twelve:
You Can Be Depressed without "Feeling Depressed"

- It is unfortunate that the word *depression* is used to describe so many different, yet sometimes overlapping, experiences.

- Yes, many people who have clinical depression feel down, sad, disappointed, and upset. One can, however, feel all of these emotions ("I'm depressed!") *without* being clinically depressed.

- The pain after a loss, for example, is a natural part of the healing process, not a sign of clinical depression. (If the pain becomes extremely severe or continues for an unusual length of time, the loss may have triggered a type of clinical depression that's known as a *melancholy depression*. When mourning becomes melancholia, or if a loss has dealt a severe blow to your self-worth, see your physician.)

- On the other hand, some people *do* have a clinical depression and *do not* feel unusual amounts of sorrow, sadness, or emotional hurt.

- Symptoms of clinical depression include insomnia; eating disturbances; difficulty concentrating, remembering, or making decisions. These are not, however, what most people call "down" or "depressing" emotions.

- If in doubt, it is best to get an objective, outside expert—your physician—to make an accurate diagnosis.

*I have secluded myself
from society;
and yet I never meant
any such thing.
I have made a captive of myself
and put me into a dungeon,
and now I cannot find the key
to let myself out.*

NATHANIEL HAWTHORNE

Thirteen:
Seeking Treatment for Depression Does Not Imply a Lack of Character, Discipline, Common Sense, or Personal Strength

- Because of the stigma of depression, many people think that seeking help implies some sort of personal lack—a lack that *should* be overcome by strength, fortitude, or gumption.

- This is not the case.

- Seeking help for an illness (*any* illness) does not imply a lack of mental, physical, emotional, or moral character.

- To the contrary, it takes great courage to admit something *may* be wrong. It is a sign of deep wisdom to consult professionals, seeking their advice and direction.

*A pessimist is one who builds
dungeons in the air.*

WALTER WINCHELL

Fourteen:
How Did Annie Hall Get Her Name?

- The original title for Woody Allen's film *Annie Hall* was *Anne Hedonia*.

- "Sometimes [depression] is mere passive joylessness and dreariness, discouragement, dejection, lack of taste and zest and spring," wrote the father of American psychology, William James, in 1902. "Professor Ribot has proposed the name *anhedonia* to designate this condition."

- Anhedonia was derived from the Greek: *an*, meaning not, and *hedone*, meaning pleasure— the inability to experience pleasure.

- If it's been a while since you've genuinely enjoyed your life (or can't relate much to the terms *enjoyment*, *pleasure*, or *fun*), that may indicate depression.

There's an old joke:
Two elderly women are
at a Catskill Mountain resort
and one of them says,
"Boy, the food at this place
is really terrible."
The other one says,
"Yeah, I know,
and such small portions."
Well, that's essentially
how I feel about life.

WOODY ALLEN

OPENING LINES TO
ANNIE HALL

Fifteen:
Other Types of Depression

- In addition to the Big Three we discussed on page 20—major depression, chronic low-grade depression (dysthymia), and manic-depression—there are some other types of depression:

  —*Seasonal Affective Disorder (SAD).* This seems to be associated with the reduction of daylight hours during winter. The treatment may be as simple as installing full-spectrum fluorescent lighting in the home and workplace. (New Yorkers have been prescribing for themselves winter trips to Miami for generations.)

  —*Postpartum Depression.* Fifty to seventy-five percent of all women, following childbirth, experience "postpartum blues." One in ten women who experience this, however, develop a postpartum *depression.* This means that from five to seven and one-half percent of all new mothers have a depression that requires treatment. Postpartum depression seems to be caused by the hormonal, physiological, and emotional vulnerabilities of this period. If the normal "postpartum blues" seem particularly severe, or they continue for more than a few weeks, discuss it with your doctor.

  —*Atypical Depression.* Atypical (*not* typical) depression has symptoms which seem to be the opposite of what was

Joy, affection, desire, pride,
humor are all drained away.
What makes life worth living
disappears slowly,
-    relentlessly
until nothing seems to be left.
Anhedonia creeps in and claims
the person who once
laughed with you,
who once hugged you,
who once loved to be
first on the hill
to catch the new powder snow.
The lights go out one by one.
It is the death of the spirit.

MARYELLEN WALSH

once thought to be a typical depression. Rather than sleeping less, people sleep more; rather than lose weight, they gain weight; rather than have low energy, they're agitated. In addition, people with atypical depression tend to be *extremely* sensitive to rejection.

—*Double Depression.* Here someone with a chronic low-grade depression (dysthymia) has a major depression as well. As we previously noted, chronic depressions can go on for years, even decades, while major depressions have a beginning, a middle, and an end. During the time one has both chronic depression and a major depression, it's a double depression.

- A psychiatrist or physician well versed in diagnosing depression will know the symptoms to look for in determining which depression you may have.

- (Please don't use this brief list to try to categorize or diagnose yourself or others. It is presented here simply to give an idea of the range and varieties depressive illness can take.)

How heavy the days are.
There is not a fire
that can warm me,
not a sun to laugh with me.
Everything base.
Everything cold and merciless.
And even the beloved dear stars
look desolately down.

HERMANN HESSE

STEPPENWOLF

Sixteen:
Delay Major Decisions—
Depression Alters Perception

- It's important to remember that when depressed, we are not perceiving the world, or ourselves, accurately. Therefore, evaluations, judgments, and decisions may be inaccurate.

- If you think you may be depressed, the only major decision to make is to get a diagnosis and, if diagnosed as depressed, to get treatment. Other major decisions can wait until the depression begins to heal.

*Only in quiet waters
things mirror themselves
undistorted.
Only in a quiet mind
is adequate
perception of the world.*

HANS MARGOLIUS

Seventeen:
The Question of Suicide

- It is very common for depressed people to have thoughts and feelings of suicide. Such thoughts and feelings are, in fact, a symptom of depression.

- For obvious reasons, however, it is important not to *act* upon suicidal thoughts or feelings.

- Sadly, fifteen percent of all depressed people will commit suicide as a result of their depression. Two-thirds of all suicides are directly related to depression.

- If you feel you even *may* act upon suicidal thoughts or feelings, call a crisis prevention line, your family doctor, a good friend, or any healthcare professional *at once*. Go to an emergency room, or call 999 and say, "I'm feeling suicidal. Please help."

- As your depression heals, life improves; you will no longer feel like committing suicide.

- Yes, life will still have its ups and downs, and you will feel your fair share of sadness, anger, grief, fear, and all the other "down" emotions. As depression heals, however, suicide will seldom seem the only solution.

- The question of suicide? Keep it a question. It's not really an answer.

Despair,
owing to some evil trick
played upon the sick brain
by the inhabiting psyche,
comes to resemble the diabolical
discomfort of being imprisoned
in a fiercely overheated room.
And because no breeze
stirs this cauldron,
because there is no escape
from this smothering confinement,
it is entirely natural that the victim
begins to think ceaselessly of oblivion.

WILLIAM STYRON

Eighteen:
The Power of Positive Thinking Crashes and Burns in the Face of Depression

- As powerful as the power of positive thoughts are, depression *biologically interferes* with the brain's ability to maintain a positive thought for any period of time. Like the farmer who casts his seed upon the rocks, all the positive thoughts in the world presented to the depressed mind will not bear fruit.

- "There are joys which long to be ours," wrote Henry Ward Beecher. "God sends ten thousand truths, which come about us like birds seeking inlet; but we are shut up to them, and so they bring us nothing, but sit and sing awhile upon the roof, and then fly away."

- Depression shuts us up.

- Overly positive, horrendously cheerful people can make a depressed person even more depressed. In fact, perhaps the *least* helpful thing one can say to a depressed person is, "Cheer up!"

- When thinking is distorted, as it is during depression, medical *treatment* is needed to till the soil so that positive thoughts can take root.

Every day,
in every way,
things are getting
worse and worse.

WILLIAM F. BUCKLEY, JR.

Nineteen:
God and Depression

- Here we use the word *God* in the broadest possible sense. Please fill in your personal belief when we use the word *God*.

- There are many misconceptions concerning God and depression. These include

    —Depression is a punishment from God.
    —To seek help for depression is to doubt God's ability to heal it.
    —If we "suffer enough," God will be pleased with us.
    —Depression is a spiritual illness; the only treatment should be God's personal intervention.

- In fact (or at least it seems a fact to *us*), God and God's benevolence come in many forms and manifest in many ways. Among these we must include modern science and the entire healing profession. (God moves in mysterious ways; psychiatrists are just one of them.)

- It is hard to find the believer who will not take penicillin for pneumonia, insulin for diabetes, or have a broken bone properly set.

- The overwhelming majority of people who are successfully treated for depression find that their faith, spiritual connection, and perception of divine goodness *increase*.

- Modern treatment of depression is a gift of God.

When I said,
"My foot is slipping,"
your love, O Lord,
supported me.
When anxiety was great
within me,
your consolation
brought joy to my soul.

PSALMS 94:18–19

Twenty:
What Causes Depression?

- Depression manifests as an imbalance in the biochemistry of the brain. This results in what some call "faulty thinking." This combination of biological imbalance and psychological distortion causes the havoc known as depression.

- A depression can be triggered—that is, set off—by any number of factors: genetic predisposition, major loss, a painful childhood, unresolved grief, stress, serious illness, economic difficulties, bad relationships, and so much more. These are, however, merely what *sets off* the depression.

- The state of "being depressed" (having a depressive illness) takes place in the brain: a biochemical imbalance in the brain and a psychological imbalance in thinking.

- Let's explore each in greater detail.

Hope is the feeling you have
that the feeling you have
isn't permanent.

JEAN KERR

Twenty-one:
The Messengers of the Brain

- The human brain is the most intricate, complex, and exquisite communication center on earth. Ten billion brain cells transmit billions of messages each second. And, as Alan Watts pointed out, "It does all this without our even thinking about it."

- The biochemical messengers of this communication are known as *neurotransmitters*. (*Neuro* refers to the brain cells and *transmitter*, to sending and receiving information.)

- When neurotransmitters are at appropriate levels, the brain functions harmoniously. We tend to feel good. We have hope, purpose, and direction. Although we certainly experience the ups and downs of life, the overall mood is one of well-being, confidence, and security.

- Although there are dozens of different neurotransmitters, research indicates that a deficiency in some of the neurotransmitters* may be one cause of depression. On the other hand, excess amounts of neurotransmitters may be a cause of the manic phase of manic-depression.

- Restoring these neurotransmitters to natural levels by way of antidepressant medication brings the brain back into harmonious functioning and a return to well-being.

* Specifically *serotonin, norepinephrine,* and *dopamine.*

*The future may teach us
how to exercise a direct
influence by means of
particular chemical substances,
upon the amount of energy
and their distribution
in the apparatus of the mind.
It may be that there are other
undreamed of possibilities
of therapy.*

SIGMUND FREUD

Twenty-two:
The Mind and Its Negative Thoughts

- Negative thoughts can play an important role in depression. Such thoughts can become a bad habit. For some, they become an addiction.

- Some common negative thoughts include

    —"I'm no good."
    —"No one understands me."
    —"Life isn't fair."
    —"I don't *dare* do that."
    —"How dare they do that?"
    —"I hate it when . . . ."
    —"I'm afraid that . . . ."
    —"I'm a failure."

- These can lead to habitual, often addictive behavior, such as

    —Overeating
    —Drug abuse
    —Alcoholism
    —Smoking
    —Compulsive gambling
    —Shoplifting
    —Sexual compulsions
    —Workaholism

- And many more.

- Habitual patterns of negative thoughts and self-destructive behavior can cause, continue, or worsen a depression.

It is hard to fight an enemy
who has outposts in your head.

SALLY KEMPTON

Twenty-three:
Which Came First?

- So, depression manifests itself as a biochemical imbalance in the brain and as negative thoughts in the mind. But where does depression begin? Which manifestation is the "first cause" of depression?

- The answer: it doesn't really matter.

- A deficiency of neurotransmitters can contribute to negative thoughts and behaviors. And, negative thoughts and behaviors can contribute to a reduction in neurotransmitters. Whichever started the depression, it becomes a downward spiral, one feeding the other into a deepening gloom.

- Which came first, then, is not important. What to *do* about depression is. Antidepressant medication helps restore the proper balance of neurotransmitters in the brain. Certain short-term therapies (most particularly Cognitive and Interpersonal therapies) teach new habits of thought and action. The medical (brain) and psychotherapeutic (mind) approaches have, individually, been successful in treating depression.

- Some prefer to approach healing from one angle; others prefer to approach it from the other. Gluttons for happiness that we are, we suggest you consider *both*. Combining therapies appears to be the most successful treatment of all.

Every excess causes a defect;
every defect an excess.

EMERSON

Twenty-four:
Depression Can Be Hereditary and "Contagious"

- Like many illnesses, depression runs in the family. Heart disease, hypertension, and depression are among the illnesses that are common to certain family trees.

- Living with someone who is chronically depressed can be depressing. When a relative or loved one has recurrent episodes of depression, there is a profound disruption of family life. Family members experience pain, exhaustion, and are more prone to depression.

- "Misery no longer loves company," Russell Baker observed. "Nowadays it insists upon it."

I was once thrown out
of a mental hospital
for depressing the other patients.

OSCAR LEVANT

Twenty-five:
Depression Related to Age

- Depressions can take place at any age. Infants can have depression, as can people well into their second century on earth.

- About six million American children under twelve have a clinical depression, much of it unrecognized and untreated. Sometimes behavior diagnosed as an Attention Deficit Disorder (children who are easily distracted, hyperactive, and have difficulty paying attention) is, in fact, depression.

- One in twenty adolescents suffers from depression. Hormonal changes, emerging identity crises, peer pressure, sexual issues, and the increased responsibility of approaching adulthood can contribute to depression. Tragically, the suicide rate among teenagers has almost tripled in one generation.

- The generation from eighteen to thirty—sometimes called Generation-X—realizes it may be the first generation in the history of the United States to be less affluent than the generation before. Many who make up Generation-X are also keenly aware of the condition of the country and planet being passed on to them. Understandably, many are not happy about it. For some individuals, this unhappiness deepens into a depression.

- The ubiquitous baby boomers—some in their forties, some in their fifties, and most in denial—find that they have *become* their parents. All the problems, crises, and attitudes they so

*He who is of
calm and happy nature
will hardly feel
the pressure of age,
but to him
who is of opposite disposition,
youth and age
are equally a burden.*

PLATO

despised in their parents have come home to roost. In addition, the post-war generation is discovering that, like Peter Pan exiled from Never-Never Land, youth is not eternal. And then there's that icky thing called *death*. All of this leads to what has been dubbed the Baby Boomer Blues.

- People over sixty-five are four times more likely to experience depression than the general population. Tragically, many elderly people are believed to have early stages of senility or Alzheimer's disease when, in fact, they have a treatable depression.

- Too often, the symptoms of depression—from physical aches and pains to poor memory— are written off as "just growing old." While certain physical and mental problems may arise due to aging, they may *also* be symptoms of depression that should be carefully evaluated by a physician.

- Above all, it is *never* normal to feel unhappy day after day, simply because you're growing older.

Nobody grows old
by merely living
a number of years.
People grow old
only by deserting their ideals.
Years wrinkle the face,
but to give up enthusiasm
wrinkles the soul.
Worry, doubt, self-interest,
fear, despair—
these are the long, long years
that bow the head and turn
the growing spirit back to dust.

WATTERSON LOWE

Twenty-six:
The Ain't-It-Awful Club

- A person can seldom experience the feelings associated with depression—misery, fear, anger, hurt, or an inability to experience pleasure—without looking for a cause.

- The symptoms of depression are often blamed on everything *but* depression.

- People look for a cause for these feelings in two places: within themselves or outside themselves.

- Those who look inward for the cause of their depressive symptoms feel blame, guilt, and shame. They are mercilessly criticized by the inner voice of depression.

- Those who look outside themselves for causes of depression tend to become angry, contemptuous, arrogant, destructive (sometimes physically), and spend a great deal of time complaining—usually to other depressed people.

- Members of the Ain't-It-Awful Club gather in bars and cocktail lounges all over the country between five and seven, when drinks are half price, and the only rule is, "You get to tell me your problems, but you have to listen to mine." For some unknown reason, this is known as the Happy Hour.

- Inappropriate blame—either inner or outer—contributes to an ever-deepening depression.

*I personally think
we developed language
because of our deep inner need
to complain.*

JANE WAGNER

Twenty-seven:
Physical Pain and Depression

- Thus far, we have been exploring the emotional pain caused by depression. Depression can cause physical pain, too.

- Physical pain can be both a symptom of and a cause of depression.

- Vague physical aches and pains that do not respond to treatment may, in fact, be a manifestation of depression. Some people feel the pain of depression primarily *physically* rather than emotionally or mentally.

- On the other hand, the chronic (long-term) physical pain caused by an accident, arthritis, back problems, burns, cancer, AIDS, or other illness can trigger a depression. Biologically, chronic pain can deplete the supply of neurotransmitters in the brain.

- To make matters worse, depression can lower the threshold of pain—pain tends to be felt more often and more intensely.

- All pain is real. Nothing we say here is to imply that the physical pain from depression is only "in your head." It is as real as any other pain, and needs to be treated.

- If you know you are depressed, do not simply write off physical aches and pains as symptoms of depression. Pain is a signal from the body that something needs attention and care. Report all physical pain to your physician.

- Those with chronic pain due to an accident or illness would do well to discuss with their physician whether depression is also present.

*Mysteriously and in ways
that are totally remote
from normal experience,
the gray drizzle of horror
induced by depression
takes on the quality
of physical pain.*

WILLIAM STYRON

Twenty-eight:
Depression Affects the Length and Quality of Life

- Obviously, the symptoms of depression on page 22 would not be a listing of what people refer to when they discuss "the quality of life."

- But on top of the pain, misery, and unproductiveness depression brings, it also brings an increase in physical illness.

- Many people with depression produce a higher-than-normal level of the hormone *cortisol*. Cortisol suppresses the immune system.

- A suppressed immune system makes one more vulnerable to infectious illness. In addition, a suppressed immune system can make one more susceptible to cancer.

- People who suffer from "poor health" may run from doctor to doctor putting out one fire after another, when the underlying cause may be depression.

- In a vicious cycle, a depression can contribute to chronic illness, and chronic illness can contribute to depression. It's often hard to tell which came first, but it's easy to see how both can feed upon each other, causing more illness, more depression, and shortening life.

- Those suffering from a chronic illness would do well to discuss with their doctor whether depression is also present.

*Heavy thoughts
bring on
physical maladies.*

MARTIN LUTHER
1483–1546

Twenty-nine:
Depression is the #1 Cause of Alcoholism, Drug Abuse, and Other Addictions

- Depression can be an all-pervasive emotional-mental-physical source of misery. It's hard to hurt so completely and for so long without seeking some relief from the pain.

- Almost any drug or distraction will do.

- Alcohol is the most commonly self-prescribed painkiller for depression. It is readily available and socially acceptable. Unfortunately, alcohol is chemically a depressant. After its brief euphoric effects, it only worsens the depression. This is especially true when alcohol is taken in the quantities some people consume in order to obtain mental and emotional oblivion.

- Drugs of all kinds—legal, illegal, over-the-counter, or prescription—are sometimes inappropriately used by depressed people for numbing specific symptoms. Alas, they do not treat the underlying cause. Uppers, downers, painkillers, tranquilizers, "getting high," and all the rest are ineffective treatment for depression. In fact, they can worsen the depression.

- We certainly aren't saying that social drinking, prescription drugs, or appropriately selected medications for either therapeutic or recreational purposes are always bad, always a sign of depression, or always cause depression. We are simply saying that *anything*—even good things—can be abused in an effort to "self-

*The problems of alcoholism
and drug addiction
have strong links to depression.
The search for highs
may often begin
as a flight from lows.*

NATHAN S. KLINE, M.D.

medicate" the symptoms of depression.

- Tobacco is both a stimulant *and* a depressant. Consequently, it can be used by smokers to regulate mood—up, down, or both. Unfortunately, nicotine is one of the most addictive substances known, and the "side effects" of smoking result in numerous illnesses and 500,000 deaths each year in the United States. Even if smoking *were* the cure for depression (which it's not) and even if tobacco *didn't* contribute to depression (which it does), the side effects alone would rule it out as a drug of choice.

- These "self-medications" need not be chemical. People have been known to abuse just about anything you can name in an effort to distract themselves from an untreated depression: food, sex, TV, gambling, work—even romance and religion.

- Anything can become a compulsion—a joyless, driven, addictive behavior. What may be good and positive in its proper place becomes not only a cover-up for the depression, but, in time, contributes to the depression itself.

- Certainly people can have compulsions without being depressed, and not all depressed people have serious compulsions. If you have a "bad habit," however, it may be worth exploring the possibility of depression with your physician.

It is a time when one's spirit
is subdued and sad,
one knows not why;
when the past seems
a storm-swept desolation,
life a vanity and a burden,
and the future
but a way to death.

MARK TWAIN

Thirty:
Eating Disorders

- Depression may contribute to eating disorders, and eating disorders may contribute to depression. It's another of those downward spirals.

  —*Anorexia nervosa* is characterized by severe weight loss, distorted body image, and an extreme fear of becoming overweight.

  —*Bulimia* is binge-eating, followed by purging—either through vomiting or laxatives. Some bulimics also have anorexia nervosa.

  —*Obesity* is caused by eating until the body is dangerously overweight.

- Depression can be an underlying cause of eating disorders. In one study, as many as three out of four bulimic individuals were depressed. The vast majority of them benefited from treatment for depression.

- Eating disorders are illnesses. They are not anyone's fault. They are not a lack of will power, character, or self-discipline.

- If depression is contributing to these illnesses, treating the depression is an important complement to treating the eating disorder.

*When one has a famishing
thirst for happiness,
one is apt
to gulp down diversions
wherever they are offered.*

ALICE CALDWELL RICE

Thirty-one:
Insomnia and Other Sleep Disorders

- Most people with depression have a sleep disorder. The most common is *insomnia*—the inability to fall asleep and stay asleep. People suffering from depression often tell their doctors, "I can't remember the last time I had a good night's sleep."

- There are basically three types of insomnia:

    —*Difficulty falling asleep*
    —*Difficulty staying asleep*, also known as *intermittent awakening*
    —*Early morning awakening*, in which one awakes at three or four o'clock in the morning and is unable to get back to sleep

- At the other end of the spectrum lies *hypersomnia*—*hyper*, for lots, and *somnia*, for sleep. People with hypersomnia can sleep ten, twelve, fourteen hours at night and still take naps during the day.

- Both insomnia and hypersomnia can indicate depression.

- Unfortunately, insomnia is sometimes inappropriately treated with sleeping pills, which do not treat the underlying depression *and* can make the depression worse. Anyone who regularly takes sleeping pills—either over-the-counter or prescription—should discuss the possibility of depression with his or her physician.

In a real dark night of the soul
it is always three o'clock
in the morning,
day after day.

F. SCOTT FITZGERALD

Thirty-two:
Fatigue

- The most common symptom of depression presented to doctors is fatigue. Certainly, fatigue has any number of physical and mental causes (mononucleosis, hepatitis, excessive workload, profound boredom), but when fatigue persists, depression should not be overlooked.

- Fatigue is more than just being occasionally tired. Tiredness is a natural phenomenon and a signal to rest. Many people with fatigue, however, awaken from a full night's sleep and still feel exhausted. Or, they may have only a few productive hours in the day.

- Procrastination, distraction, and lack of motivation are often manifestations of fatigue.

- Depression also brings a mental fatigue—the mind is simply "tired," and one has difficulty thinking, concentrating, or making decisions.

- Emotional fatigue is often felt as "I can't take any more," "Leave me alone," and often manifests as irritability or withdrawal.

- For many, the lifting of fatigue that follows the successful treatment of depression can transform their lives.

As the lack of sleep
wore me down,
a sense of hopelessness
enveloped me.
I knew that nothing I did
could change the situation.
There was nothing I <u>could</u> do.
I was convinced that I was laboring
under some kind of curse
so that any efforts of my own
to fight this situation
were foredoomed to failure.

PERCY KNAUTH

Thirty-three:
Depression Destroys Relationships

- Depression impairs the ability to care and be cared for, give and receive, love and be loved.

- Depression can significantly interfere with *all* relationships—with friends, co-workers, bosses, employees, children, parents, spouses, lovers, and even one's relationship with self, God, and life.

- Relationships are an excellent mirror as to how we are doing. If the relationships in one's life seem deeply troubled, perhaps it's because that person is deeply troubled. The trouble may be depression.

*It's surprising
how many persons
go through life
without ever recognizing that
their feelings toward other people
are largely determined
by their feelings toward themselves,
and if you're not
comfortable within yourself,
you can't be
comfortable with others.*

SYDNEY J. HARRIS

Thirty-four:
Romanticizing Depression

- In days of old (prior to the mid-1950s) there were few effective treatments for depression. People, however, knew depression well.

- Depression is as old as humankind. "The Man Who Was Tired of Life" is the title of a poem written in 1990—that's 1990 *B.C.*

- What can poets and philosophers do when they have a malady that has no treatment? Romanticize it, of course. Thus sprang the belief that depression was essential to the development of a human being.

- "All artists today," said Lawrence Durrell, "are expected to cultivate a little fashionable unhappiness."

- In 1621, Robert Burton observed that nothing was "so sweet as melancholy," and Maurice Maeterlinck mused in 1896, "The value of ourselves is but the value of our melancholy and our disquiet."

- Some artistic or intellectual people avoid treatment for fear of losing their creative sensibilities. It may be difficult to communicate to them that ongoing suffering does not bring about deepening wisdom, perception of life's "true reality," or creative achievement.

- Depression is an illness, and it is no more noble today to suffer from it than it would be to suffer from untreated scurvy, syphilis, or goiter—three illnesses that, like depression, had no known cure a century or so ago.

Suffering is overrated.

BILL VEECK

Thirty-five:
The Stigma of Depression

- The flip side of romanticizing depression is the enormous social stigma of depression and the treatment of depression itself.

- Some believe that depression is the first step on a short walk to the loony bin. Others believe that the treatment of depression is just too hip to be true.

- *Newsweek* stated on its February 7, 1994, cover, "Shy? Forgetful? Anxious? Fearful? Obsessed? How science will let you change your personality with a pill." *Newsweek* suggests that shyness, forgetfulness, anxiety, fear, and obsession are part of one's *personality*. They are also possible symptoms of depression.

- As long as people *identify* with their depression as though it were some part of their *self*, ("It's just the way I am"), they're not likely to seek diagnosis and treatment.

- The major problem *by far* with treating depression in this country is undertreatment.

- Nevertheless, some people mock antidepressant treatments as a trendy fad, making snide comments about "Vitamin P" or the "Prozac personality." (In fact, people successfully treated for depression report they feel *more themselves*.)

- Please don't let any of this media chatter interfere with your seeking a diagnosis, treatment, and healing.

*Physical and social functioning
are impaired by depression
to a greater degree
than by hypertension,
diabetes, angina,
arthritis, gastrointestinal diseases,
lung problems, or back ailments.*

JOSÉ M. SANTIAGO, M.D.
JOURNAL OF CLINICAL PSYCHOLOGY
November, 1993

Thirty-six:
Why Depression _Must_ Be Treated

- That may sound like a rather strong statement— as you may have noticed, we seldom use the word _must_ (at least in print). The statement, however, is not ours. It comes from the U.S. Department of Health and Human Services.

- Major depression, untreated, can last six months to a year. It then goes away. (One cycle of a major depression—its beginning, middle, and end—is known as an _episode._) Without treatment, half the people who have one depressive episode will have another. After two episodes, the chances of having a third episode are even greater. After three episodes, the chances of having a fourth depression are ninety percent.

- Chronic low-grade depression (dysthymia) may not have any seriously debilitating symptoms, but it can interfere with work, family, and almost all other aspects of life. Untreated, it can last for years, decades, or a lifetime. Dysthymia, in fact, becomes a "ground of being," and it's hard for a person with a long-term depression to even imagine another way of feeling, thinking, or behaving. Without treatment, the chances are that chronic depression will continue and, most likely, worsen.

- Manic-depression, untreated, continues. The highs become increasingly unstable, and the lows become increasingly painful. The sudden shifts from mania to depression become more

Recurrence is sure.
What the mind suffered
last week,
or last year,
it does not suffer now;
but it will suffer again
next week or next year.
Happiness is not
a matter of events;
it depends upon
the tides of the mind.

ALICE MEYNELL

frequent and debilitating.

- Many people postpone treatment, thinking the depression will simply "go away." This may or may not take place. As with any serious illness, it is always advisable to seek treatment.

- Depression, like any major illness, is better treated sooner than later. Treatment tends to be more successful the earlier it is begun.

- And, most importantly, the earlier the illness is treated, the sooner the suffering ends, and the sooner one returns to life, loves, friends, and full productivity.

- Please don't postpone your healing.

*You become a pessimist
—a demonic,
elemental,
bestial pessimist—
only when life
has been defeated
many times in its fight
against depression.*

E. M. CIORAN

Thirty-seven:
Treatment for Depression
Is a <u>Natural</u> Process

- Both pillars of treatment for depression—antidepressant medications for the brain and psychotherapy for the mind—are, for the most part, *natural* processes.

- Psychotherapy involves mostly *talking*—a natural process. There is no "brainwashing," and you will not be told you *must* do anything (contrary to our previous chapter).

- Antidepressant medications simply restore the brain's *natural* levels of certain *naturally* produced neurotransmitters. "Synthetic" neurotransmitters are not added. Antidepressants simply balance the supply of naturally produced neurotransmitters.

- For example, antidepressants such as Prozac, Paxil, and Zoloft tell the brain not to break down the neurotransmitter *serotonin* too soon. This restores serotonin to its natural levels, and the brain can function harmoniously again.*

- The most recently introduced antidepressant (as of spring 1994) is Effexor. Effexor prevents the premature breakdown of *two* neurotransmitters, serotonin and norepinephrine. The

---

* Antidepressants that act in this way are known as serotonin reuptake inhibitors. *Reuptake* means the body is "taking up" serotonin and breaking it down. *Inhibitors* slow the action of this reuptake, allowing serotonin to remain at natural levels. Hence: serotonin reuptake inhibitors, or SRIs.

*In view of the intimate
connection between things
physical and mental,
we may look forward to the day
when paths of knowledge
will be opened up
leading from organic biology
and chemistry to the field of
neurotic phenomena.*

SIGMUND FREUD

latter has been associated with physical energy and heightened mental clarity. Hence, Effexor has been dubbed "Prozac with a boost."

- You don't "feel" antidepressant medications in the way you feel other mood-altering drugs such as alcohol, tranquilizers, or amphetamines. The improvements experienced with antidepressants seem to come from re-establishing natural levels of certain neurotransmitters produced by the brain.

- Lithium, the primary antidepressant medication prescribed for manic-depression, is a simple salt. Its beneficial effect on those with manic-depression was discovered by Dr. John Cade in 1949—although the physician Galen, who practiced around 200 A.D., advised bathing manic patients in alkaline springs. Perhaps the salt, lithium carbonate, was absorbed through the skin and that calmed the manic patient.

- All medications involve some degree of risk and have, for some, side effects. The risks and side effects of the newer antidepressant drugs are comparatively low.

- "Antidepressant drugs are not habit forming or addictive," the National Institutes of Health tells us.

- The potential rewards far outweigh the risks.

*He who postpones
the hour of living
is like
the rustic who waits
for the river
to run out
before he crosses.*

HORACE

FIRST CENTURY B.C.

Thirty-eight:
Your Treatment Is Unique to You

- Your treatment for depression is uniquely yours. Although you'll be receiving guidance, diagnosis, advice, and suggestions from one or more healthcare professionals, your treatment is, fundamentally, your own.

- Among other things, you must choose who the healthcare individual or individuals will be. And, you must choose from the various courses of treatment presented.

- Don't become a sheep. Become educated. Ask questions.

- Your healing is in your hands.

- Perhaps most importantly, it's up to you to follow through on the treatment you choose. If you take antidepressant medications, don't just take them until you "feel better"; take them for as long as your doctor recommends. If you agree to a certain number of therapeutic sessions, fulfill your commitment.

- To the degree that's possible, enjoy your healing. If you've suffered from depression for a long time, you may discover depths and riches within yourself you have not known for years—perhaps ever. This can be a challenging but exciting journey.

Happiness,
that grand mistress
of the ceremonies
in the dance of life,
impels us through
all its mazes and meanderings,
but leads none of us
by the same route.

CHARLES CALEB COLTON

*Men ought to know
that from nothing else
but the brain
come joys,
delights,
laughter and sports,
grief,
despondency
and lamentations.*

HIPPOCRATES

Part II
Healing the Brain

Current research points to an imbalance of biochemicals in the brain as the seat of depression. Recent medical breakthroughs have led to effective treatments and cures for depression for the first time in history. These are what we'll explore in this part of the book, along with important healthcare tips to speed your healing.

Thirty-nine:
Choose a Doctor

- The health professional to *diagnose* and *medically* treat depression is the physician (an M.D.).* As we shall explore shortly, other physical illnesses can have symptoms similar to depression, or may be the cause of depression itself. It is one of the doctor's jobs to rule out those illnesses when symptoms of depression are present.

- Psychiatrists are the physicians best suited to diagnose and treat depression. Psychiatrists are, first and foremost, medical doctors. They have, in addition, three years of training in the workings of the brain and mind. Many psychiatrists now specialize in treating depression.

- According to a 1993 survey performed by the RAND Corporation, fewer than half the general practitioners ("family doctors") treating depressed patients had spent more than *three minutes* discussing their patient's symptoms before determining if the patient had a depression. While diagnosing depression usually takes no more than one or two fifty-minute consultations, three minutes is obviously far too brief. This may explain why general prac-

---

* As we shall discuss in Part III, the professional who may be best suited to provide psychotherapeutic treatment for depression is a psychologist or other qualified mental health practitioner. In this part of the book, we are looking at *medical* diagnosis and treatment.

Never go to a doctor
whose office plants
have died.

ERMA BOMBECK

titioners fail to diagnose depression accurately about half the time. (They tend not to find a depression when one exists.)

- More and more general practitioners, however, are becoming well versed in the treatment of depression and are taking the necessary time to do a proper diagnostic evaluation. The psychiatrist, then, is certainly not the only physician who can successfully diagnose and treat depression.

- Most important, you want to find a competent physician with whom you feel *comfortable*, someone you can trust with the most intimate details of your life. You must give thorough, complete information about all aspects of your life if the doctor is to make an accurate diagnosis and prescribe the most effective treatment. In addition, the physician you choose to work with you must provide emotional support, encouragement, and guidance. It's important that you can feel his or her compassion and caring.

- If your family doctor or healthcare professional does not specialize in the diagnosis and treatment of depression, he or she will probably be able to recommend a psychiatrist who does. There is no need to choose the first recommendation. Sometimes "interviewing" two or three prospective psychiatrists is in order.

*Macbeth: Canst thou not
minister to a mind diseased,
Pluck from the memory
a rooted sorrow,
Raze out the troubles of the brain,
and with some sweet
oblivious antidote
Cleanse the stuffed bosom
of that perilous stuff
Which weighs upon the heart?*

*Doctor: Therein the patient
Must minister to himself.*

SHAKESPEARE

Forty:
The Diagnosis of Depression

- Diagnosing depression—from the patient's point of view—is an uncomplicated, straightforward procedure.

- There will probably be forms to fill out (aren't there always?) about your medical and personal history.

- Because depression tends to run in families, you may be asked to answer a few questions about your family medical history.

- Your doctor might also perform what's called a medical workup, to rule out physical illnesses that can first appear as a depression. These can include low thyroid, mononucleosis, anemia, diabetes (half of the fifteen million people with diabetes in this country don't know they have it), adrenal insufficiency, and hepatitis, among others. (Most of these can be determined by a simple blood test.)

- You'll be asked about medications you are taking or have recently taken. Certain prescription drugs (for example, high blood pressure medications, birth control pills, or steroids) and over-the-counter drugs (such as diet or sleeping pills) can sometimes cause depression.

- It's also a good idea to provide your diagnosing physician with a *complete* list of all vitamins, minerals, herbs, amino acids, or recreational drugs you may have taken in the past year. (Understandably, you may not want to

*If this essential
core of the person
is denied or suppressed,
he gets sick
sometimes in obvious ways,
sometimes in subtle ways,
sometimes immediately,
sometimes later.*

ABRAHAM MASLOW

write down some of the illegal substances, but *do* tell your diagnosing physician when in the privacy of your consultation.)

- Your medical exam should include a physical, especially if you haven't had one recently.

- Mostly, though, arriving at a diagnosis will involve *talking*. You'll tell the doctor which symptoms of depression you think you have. You can ask the doctor whether what *you* are experiencing qualifies as a symptom or not. The doctor will also ask you some questions, which, of course, should be answered as frankly and completely as possible.

- After reviewing your personal, family, and medical history, and the results of all tests, your doctor may diagnose depression.

- Rather than feeling dread, most people feel relieved. *Finally*, there is a single, medical explanation for a great many frustrating, debilitating problems.

- At this point, your doctor will recommend a course of treatment. In most cases, this will include antidepressant medication and psychotherapy.

*Psychiatry is
the art of teaching people
how to stand
on their own two feet
while reclining on couches.*

SIGMUND FREUD

Forty-one:
Antidepressant Medications

- There are roughly a dozen antidepressant medications from which you and your doctor can choose. As previously mentioned, none of them is addictive or habit-forming. They are generally safe when taken as prescribed.

- Although various types of antidepressants work in different ways, the overall effect is the same: balancing the neurotransmitters in the brain, thus restoring harmony to brain functioning.

- Antidepressant medications become effective gradually. Although some people notice an improvement within days, some take as long as eight weeks to feel the maximum benefits of the medication. During this time, patience and perseverance are the key.

- Some patients decide after a few days or weeks, "This isn't working for me," and stop. Others experience side effects, fail to tell their doctor about them, and stop. Both of these responses are a mistake.

- Communicate *all* effects—especially problems—to your doctor. If the problem is especially troublesome, call *at once*. Don't wait until your next appointment. Your doctor may then prescribe a different antidepressant. If, however, your doctor suggests continuing with the medication as prescribed, please do so. Most side effects disappear within two to three weeks, or, when compared with the positive results of medication, eventually seem minimal.

The human body experiences
a powerful gravitational pull
in the direction of hope.
That is why the patient's hopes
are the physician's
secret weapon.
They are the hidden ingredients
in any prescription.

NORMAN COUSINS

Forty-two:
Side Effects

- Most people who take antidepressants experience few, if any, side effects. Those who do have mild side effects. This is especially true of the newer antidepressants (Prozac, Paxil, Zoloft, and Effexor).

- Your physician will let you know which side effects to look for with the particular antidepressant(s) you are taking.

- As previously mentioned, most antidepressants' side effects disappear on their own within two or three weeks.

- Seldom are side effects severe enough to necessitate switching medications. If you do need to change, however, take heart: there are several other antidepressants equally effective, but without the same troublesome side effects.

- Most important, do not change your medication or dosage on your own. Contact your doctor.

- Do not take any additional drugs—either over-the-counter, prescription, or recreational—without first checking with your healthcare provider. Drugs that, when taken alone, are relatively harmless can become dangerous—even deadly—when taken with some antidepressants. *Always* check with your doctor.

- Whatever the side effects may be, it is usually more harmful to have a depression than to take antidepressant medication.

How to gain,
how to keep,
how to recover
happiness
is in fact
for most men
at all times
the secret motive
of all they do,
and of all they are
willing to endure.

WILLIAM JAMES

Forty-three:
The Prozac Rumors

- It seems that whenever the subject of depression and antidepressant medications arises, the discussion turns to Prozac. Frankly, Prozac has "a bad rep."

- It is completely undeserved. Since its release in 1987, ten million people have taken Prozac. The vast, *vast* majority of them have found it to be an effective treatment for depression, with few side effects. (In fact, Prozac has fewer side effects than almost any other antidepressant.*)

- Naturally, in studying a group of ten million people doing *anything*, some aberrant behavior is likely to be found.

- A certain religious group—for whatever reason—decided to "get" Eli Lilly, the manufacturer of Prozac. The group spent millions of dollars publicizing the aberrant behavior (murders, suicides) of a handful of those ten million.

- Since then, elaborate studies—reported in everything from the *American Journal of Psychiatry* to "60 Minutes"—show that Prozac, in and of itself, does not cause a greater likelihood of aberrant behavior.

---

* We aren't here to push Prozac. Its brother and sister antidepressants, Zoloft and Paxil; its energetic close cousin, Effexor; and their sleepy buddy, Trazadone, are all excellent medications. Even the "older" antidepressants—Sinequan, Elavil, Nardil, etc.—have their place. You and your doctor working together will choose which one is right for you.

It is estimated
that ten million people
around the world
have taken Prozac,
five million of them right here
in the United States.
That's more
than the total populations
of Idaho, Montana, Wyoming,
North Dakota, South Dakota,
and Nebraska.

OPRAH WINFREY
"THE OPRAH WINFREY SHOW"
March 7, 1994

Forty-four:
The Right Medication and Dosage

- Due to the delay between starting antidepressants and seeing results, it may take a while for your doctor and you to arrive at the proper medication and dosage for you.

- Be patient with this process. During the initial phase of treatment, you may require more frequent consultations with your doctor.

- People respond differently to specific antidepressants. One person may find antidepressant A highly effective, while another person may find it only marginally effective. The other person, however, may find that antidepressant B works wonders, while the antidepressant A fan finds antidepressant B ineffective.

- The same is true of side effects. Antidepressant A may work fine, but have a disagreeable side effect, while antidepressant B may work just as well, and have no side effects.

- Although it may take a while, when you and your doctor discover the antidepressant and dosage that work best for you, it will be worth it.

*Instant gratification
takes too long.*

CARRIE FISHER

Forty-five:
"You're Not Dealing with Your Pain!"

- Some people seem morally opposed to antidepressant medication. They have a firm belief that pain must be *dealt with*, experienced, analyzed, categorized, and, at all costs, must *not* be avoided.

- These people, it seems, are confusing antidepressants with tranquilizers or painkillers.

- Antidepressants do not numb the body, mind, or emotions. On the contrary, they usually make a person more perceptive and aware of feelings.

- The suffering of depression is not the ordinary occasional pain of living. Suffering, in fact, interferes with the processing of, and taking appropriate action about, pain. Pain is a signal that something is not right. Far from covering this pain, antidepressants help you deal with it more effectively.

- People being treated for depression often find that the clarity of mind, relief of emotional suffering, and increased energy allow them to clear up problems—mental, physical, and emotional—that had been festering for years.

- Antidepressant medications, then, are not an escape, a cover-up, or a short circuit for life's difficulties. They are a medicine to heal disease and end suffering. They often make psychotherapy more effective.

*Some patients
feel guilty about
achieving recovery
with medication.
They have been
thoroughly indoctrinated
in the idea
that emotional disturbance
must reflect
psychic ills,
and they expect the treatment
to require a prolonged,
painful search
of their unconscious.*

NATHAN S. KLINE, M.D.

Forty-six:
A Good Night's Sleep

- So many people with depression experience difficulty in sleeping that—as with many other symptoms of depression—it's hard to tell whether insomnia contributed to the depression or depression contributed to the insomnia. The answer, in many cases, is both.

- Many people find that as treatment progresses they return to normal sleep cycles, which is healing in itself.

- If, after taking antidepressants for a while, you find your sleep has not returned to normal, it may be that the particular antidepressant you take has the unwanted side effect of insomnia. You may want to discuss with your doctor the possibility of a bedtime dose of an antidepressant that has sleepiness as one of its side effects. These antidepressants are not sleeping pills. When taken at bedtime, however, the side effect of sleepiness— which can obviously be a detriment during the day—becomes an added blessing.

- Sleeping pills can be easily abused and are particularly dangerous for a depressed patient. Sedatives actually disrupt your normal sleep patterns and can quickly become addicting.

- If you are already taking an over-the-counter or prescription sleeping medication, ask your doctor if it's advisable to switch you to an antidepressant at bedtime. These are often not only more effective for the depressed person, but allow him or her to avoid sleeping pills,

Go to bed.
What you're staying up for
isn't worth it.

ANDY ROONEY

which can interfere with the successful treatment of depression. As always, check with your doctor.

- Sleep is a significant part of the healing process—it is the time for your body, emotions, brain, and mind to restore themselves to proper functioning.

- Sleep is the guardian of health.

How do people go to sleep?
I'm afraid I've lost the knack.
I might try busting myself
smartly over the temple
with the nightlight.
I might repeat to myself,
slowly and soothingly,
a list of quotations beautiful
from minds profound;
if I can remember
any of the damn things.

DOROTHY PARKER

Forty-seven:
Nutritional Supplements

- Good nutrition, plus taking vitamin and mineral supplements, supports the healing of your brain and body. A nutrition-conscious doctor can test you for nutritional deficiencies and treat these appropriately.

- Consider taking a vitamin B-complex twice daily. Deficiencies of B_1, B_2, and B_6 can cause depression. Vitamin B_{12} deficiency can cause depression, neurological problems, and anemia. You may need to take the B_{12} under your tongue or as a "B_{12} shot" because this vitamin is absorbed poorly from the diet.

- Vitamin C twice daily helps combat stress and strengthens your immune system.

- A daily multimineral supplement is also helpful because a deficiency of zinc, iron, magnesium, or manganese can contribute to depression.

- *Excess* sugar, white flour, alcohol, and caffeine deplete your energy and can contribute to depression.

- Drink lots of water—at least eight 8-ounce glasses a day.

- Especially among the elderly, deficiencies of vitamins and minerals contribute to not only depression, but less-than-optimal mental performance.

- In general, vitamin/mineral supplements are better purchased at a health food store than the corner drug store.

*Everything you see
I owe to spaghetti.*

SOPHIA LOREN

Forty-eight:
Treat Your Body Well

- Anything you've learned that promotes the strengthening, flexibility, and endurance of your body will almost invariably support your overall healing and well-being.

- Exercise—particularly aerobic exercise—produces *endorphins*, which are the body's natural antidepressants. Bicycling, swimming, or even a good brisk walk can do wonders.

- Other physical activities—such as yoga, stretching, dancing, tai chi—are excellent ways to loosen the body, relieve stress, and get energy moving again.

- It's hard to overestimate the healing powers of a hot bath. If you're a typical "shower power" American, making that a ten-minute hot bath could have soothing results.

- Even more deeply relaxing is massage.

- Do more of whatever activities you personally find nurturing and enjoyable: walks in nature, viewing art, listening to good music, watching your favorite movies, gardening.

- One of the most common outcomes of a depressive illness is a mistreated body. Now is the time to treat your body well. The more you learn to treat yourself well now, the less treatment you'll need down the road.

My grandmother
started walking
five miles a day
when she was sixty.
She's ninety-five now,
and we don't know
where the hell she is.

ELLEN DEGENERIS

The mind is its own place,
and in itself can make
a Heav'n of Hell,
or a Hell of Heav'n.

JOHN MILTON
PARADISE LOST
1667

Part III

Healing the Mind

The second approach to healing depression—
co-equal with healing the brain—is healing
the mind. Extensive research has shown that
two short-term therapies, *Cognitive Therapy* and
Interpersonal Therapy, are highly effective in
the treatment of depression.

After a brief discussion of these potent therapies, we will present *our* favorite skills to heal
the mind and enjoy a happier, more productive life. (These are offered as an adjunct to,
not a substitute for, Cognitive/Interper-
sonal Therapy.)

Forty-nine:
Psychotherapy as Education

- Psychotherapy has changed considerably in the past decade. The stereotype most people have of lying on a couch for the fifty-minute hour while a dispassionate therapist sits silently taking notes has almost disappeared.

- Therapy—especially in the treatment of depression—has become much more *educational*.

- *Education* comes from the Latin word *educare*, which means to draw forth from within. A good therapist actively draws from within you things you may have known about yourself and forgotten, things you may have never known about yourself, or things that you knew to be true but, for whatever reason, disregarded.

- In addition, a therapist teaches new skills for living a more productive, satisfying, and loving life.

- Depressed people sometimes do things that make them even more depressed because *no one ever taught them any other way*.

- An important part of therapy, then, is learning other ways.

*I know of no
more encouraging fact
than the unquestionable
ability of man to elevate his life
by a conscious endeavor.*

THOREAU

Fifty:
Cognitive Therapy

- Cognitive Therapy was developed by psychiatrist Aaron T. Beck, M.D.

- The word *cognitive* relates to how we perceive and think. For example, the word *recognize* means simply to *re* (do again) *cognize* (perceive)—to cognize something we have cognized before. Descartes's famous phrase, "I think, therefore I am," is, in fact, a bad translation. A better translation would be, "I cognize, therefore I am."

- Simply put, the way we perceive the world is the way we respond to the world. If our cognition of life is negative, our thoughts, feelings, and actions will be negative.

- Cognitive Therapy identifies a person's distorted cognitions (perceptions and evaluations) and "reframes" them in a more accurate, factual light. Cognitive Therapy is *not* positive thinking—it simply seeks what's *genuine*, what's *real*, about one's life.

- Depression distorts perception. The depressed person perceives life through a glass darkly. Cognitive Therapy does not add rose-colored glasses: its goal is clear glass, which allows the world to be perceived accurately—both its good and its bad.

- Dr. Beck's therapeutic method is outlined in the book, *Feeling Good* by David D. Burns, M.D.

If we see things as negative,
we are likely to feel negative
and behave in a negative way.

AARON T. BECK, M.D.

Fifty-one:
Interpersonal Therapy

- A depressive illness colors how a person thinks, feels, and reacts toward a spouse, lover, friend, boss, co-worker, parent, or child. Troubled relationships are the rule in depression.

- Interpersonal Therapy was developed by psychiatrist Gerald Klerman, M.D., of Harvard, and Myrna Weissman, Ph.D., of Yale as a short-term therapy to help people identify and resolve their difficulties with others.*

- Whereas Cognitive Therapy focuses on perception and reaction to those perceptions, Interpersonal Therapy lays an extra emphasis on communication skills. Interpersonal Therapy and Cognitive Therapy have so many overlapping concepts and work so well together, many therapists have combined both into Cognitive/Interpersonal Therapy.

- Both Cognitive and Interpersonal Therapy deal with your habits of thought, feeling, and behavior as they are *now*, not what happened somewhere *back then* in your childhood. The origin of the pattern is not as important as the pattern itself and how to turn that pattern into one that elevates rather than depresses.

---

* *Interpersonal Psychotherapy of Depression* is the book written by Dr. Klerman and Dr. Weissman.

*Everybody forgets
the basic thing:
people are not
going to love you
unless you love them.*

PAT CARROLL

Fifty-two:
Acknowledging Two Pioneers

- We would be remiss if we did not mention two people whose work laid the foundation for the success of Cognitive and Interpersonal therapies. They are Albert Ellis, Ph.D., and Arnold Lazarus, Ph.D.

- Albert Ellis is the founder of Rational-Emotive Therapy. It is described brilliantly in his book, *How To Stubbornly Refuse to be Miserable About Anything . . . Yes, ANYTHING*.

- The idea behind Rational-Emotive Therapy is this: there are three aspects of life—(a) what really happens, (b) what we perceive about what happens, and (c) how we react. The majority of our difficulties, according to Dr. Ellis, come at point (b): what we perceive. By rationally, factually comparing our perceptions and reactions with what actually happened, we become more effective at (c): our reaction and action.

- Dr. Arnold Lazarus is the father of Multimodal Therapy. This looks at what one is thinking, feeling, and doing that is not productive, and teaches proven, effective strategies for reversing them. For example, Dr. Lazarus maintains that many people are *de*pressed because they have an inability to *ex*press. Whether the depressed expression is tenderness, assertiveness, joy, anger, or love, learning appropriate expression is valuable in the treatment of depression.

- Dr. Lazarus's most recent book is *Don't Believe It for a Minute*.

*Do you find yourself
in the same unhappy situation
again and again,
wondering where
you went wrong
and why it happened again?
It's not always just bad luck—
it may be bad ideas.*

ARNOLD A. LAZARUS, PH.D.

Fifty-three:
Psychiatrist, Psychologist, or Both?

- In some cases, you may choose the psychiatrist who is treating the medical aspect of your depression to also guide you through Cognitive/Interpersonal Therapy. This has the advantage of combining your therapy and medical visits into one.

- Or you may choose to have a psychiatrist or general practitioner diagnose, prescribe antidepressants, and monitor medical progress, *and* have a psychologist or other mental health professional provide the psychotherapy.

- A psychiatrist has more medical training, and a psychologist has more psychological training. This gives you two people with different, but overlapping, specialties working closely together on your healing.

- More and more psychologists and psychiatrists are joining together to treat depression in a "team" approach. (Keep in mind, however, that you are not stuck with either member of the team—*any* psychiatrist and *any* therapist you choose can work together on your healing.)

- Most importantly, you must feel trust, confidence, and comfort with your therapist so that you can express and explore whatever you need to in order to fully heal and grow.

*The greatest mistake in
the treatment of diseases
is that there are
physicians for the body
and physicians for the soul,
although the two
cannot be separated.*

PLATO

Fifty-four:
Books, Tapes, and Videos

- Books and tapes (both audio and video) can be excellent sources for learning new skills, ideas, and ways of looking at life. The use of books and tapes as an adjunct to therapy is growing more and more popular.

- This even has a name: *bibliotherapy*. (*Biblio* means book in Latin. Fortunately, there is no Latin word for *tape*, so there is no *tapiotherapy*.) We like James Burke's idea that a book is like holding another's mind in your hands.

- Audiotapes are especially useful because you can listen to them while you drive, jog, walk, or even clean house.

- The advent of videotapes has made thousands of movies, documentaries, and other inspirational and educational material conveniently available.

- So, here are Harold's and Peter's ten favorite books or tapes about learning life's lessons.

Rules for the list: Naturally, we weren't allowed to choose each other's books or tapes—that would have left room for very few other books. Nevertheless, we *do* recommend each other's books (Please see the list on the opening pages of this book.). For more titles on depression, please see the list at the end of this book, "Recommended Reading on Depression." Finally, we did not select any materials referred to elsewhere in this book.

Harold's List

- Concept: Synergy audiotapes by Lazaris, especially *Handling Depression, Beyond Struggle: The Magic of Being Good Enough, Ending Shame*, and *Overcoming the Dark Law*. For more information, call 1–800–678–2356.
- *What You Feel, You Can Heal*, by John Gray, Ph.D.
- *Health & Fitness Excellence*, by Robert Cooper, Ph.D.
- *All in the Family* (television sitcom), produced by Norman Lear
- *Nuclear Evolution*, by Christopher Hills, Ph.D.
- *Healing the Shame That Binds You*, by John Bradshaw
- *SeinLanguage*, by Jerry Seinfeld
- *The Conduct of Life*, by Ralph Waldo Emerson
- *The Prophet*, by Kahlil Gibran
- *Be Here Now*, by Ram Dass

Peter's List

- Meditation for Loving Yourself (audiotape), by John-Roger, 1–800–LIFE–101
- *THE BOOK on the Taboo Against Learning Who You Truly Are*, by Alan Watts (or any of Alan Watts's audiotapes, available from Electronic University, 1–800–969–2887)
- *Sunday in the Park with George* (Broadway show, available on videocassette, CD, audiocassette)
- *Airborne* by William F. Buckley, Jr.
- *Field of Dreams* (movie)
- *The Virtue of Selfishness*, by Ayn Rand
- Any "Far Side" collection by Gary Larson
- *Illusions*, by Richard Bach
- All the words in red from a Red Letter Edition of the first four books of the New Testament by Matthew, Mark, Luke, and John; New International Version
- *How to Become a Virgin* and *The Naked Civil Servant*, by Quentin Crisp

Fifty-five:
Personal Growth

- With this point, we begin sharing with you some of our favorite personal growth techniques.

- These are simply a gathering of ideas and activities you might like to try. Experiment with them. Play with them. Modify them to your needs and preferences. If they work for you, take them; they're yours. If they don't work for you, move on to techniques that do.

- Again, these suggestions are *not* a review of Cognitive/Interpersonal Therapy, nor are they the outline for Bloomfield/McWilliams Depression Therapy. And again, doing the techniques in this book is *not* a substitute for working with a professional in Cognitive/Interpersonal Therapy.

- Frankly, we do not believe that depression can be successfully treated from a book. The downward spiral of depression requires, we believe, professional intervention at both the biological and the psychological levels.

*Try a thing you haven't done
three times.
Once,
to get over the fear of doing it.
Twice,
to learn how to do it.
And a third time,
to figure out
whether you like it or not.*

VIRGIL THOMSON

ADVICE GIVEN AT AGE 93

Fifty-six:
Flexibility

- One of the hallmarks of depression is rigid, inflexible thinking.

- Words such as *must, should, never, bad, have to,* and *ought to* create emotional states (anger, fear, hurt, guilt, and unworthiness), which, naturally, tend to contribute to depression.

- Using the words listed above sets up a battle of absolutes within ourselves: bad vs. good, right vs. wrong, light vs. dark. This mental and emotional battle zone often becomes the ground of being from which we perceive and act in the world. We declare war on the world—although we are *firmly* convinced that the world has declared war on us. As in all wars, we are overcome by fear and anger.

- Not only is this a depressing way to live; it's phenomenally inaccurate. *The world does what it does,* no matter *how* depressed we become about it.

- Life is lived on the continuum between good *and* bad, right *and* wrong, light *and* dark.

- Replacing the rigid words above with more flexible (and accurate) words such as *often, sometimes, seldom, either, or,* and *both,* makes life a lot more realistic—and livable. Strive for excellence, not perfection. Practice tolerance, not insistence. Live in a world of preferences, not demands. Say, "I'd like," or "I want," rather than "I need," or "I must have . . . ."

- Life is not a struggle, it's a wiggle.

*Our best friends
and our worst enemies
are our thoughts.
A thought can do us more good
than a doctor or a banker
or a faithful friend.
It can also do us
more harm than a brick.*

DR. FRANK CRANE

Fifty-seven:
Exaggerating Is <u>Absolutely</u> the <u>Worst</u> <u>Thing</u> You Can Do, and It Can <u>Kill</u> <u>You</u> If You Don't Stop It <u>Completely</u>— <u>Right</u> <u>Now</u>!!!

- Look at the word *exaggerate*. It has too many g's, doesn't it? It only needs one g to get by. That's what we do when we exaggerate: we add extra g's. The *g-force*, of course, is the weight of gravity. Adding extra g's presses down on us, making us depressed.

- *Wasn't that first point the dumbest, stupidest, most juvenile and insultingly <u>unprofessional</u> description of how exaggeration worsens depression that you've <u>ever</u> <u>seen</u>?!*

- And so exaggeration goes. We take an idea or event and mentally blow it out of all proportion. The emotions soon follow suit. Emotions react to what the mind tells them. If we are disappointed and our mental response is, "You're killing me!" the emotions respond as though we are *literally* being killed. That's a fairly strong emotional reaction.

- Don't exaggerate in the *other* direction, either. If you're disappointed, it's fine. Don't try to kid yourself by thinking, "Oh, it really doesn't matter." If it matters to you, it matters.

- Strive for *accuracy*—a word that has a lot of c's in it. That will keep your mind and emotional responses more appropriate. C what we mean?

I have bad reflexes.
I was once run over
by a car
being pushed
by two guys.

WOODY ALLEN

Fifty-eight:
Observe Yourself

- The next time you're upset, take a step back—mentally—and *listen* to your thoughts. If you're speaking to someone, *hear* what you're saying. If you're doing something, *observe* your actions. When you objectively stand back and monitor your thoughts, words, and actions, you'll see where a good deal of your negativity is coming from.

- Look for *shoulds, have-tos, musts*. Look for exaggerations. Look for assumptions you've made. (You've probably heard the old saying: "To *assume* is to make an *ass* out of *u* and *me*.") Look for judgments.

- Then see where all this negative thinking gets you: the negative feelings, the words that don't truly reflect *you*, the ineffective actions.

- Also notice what you're *ignoring*. What are the good things going on that you're paying absolutely no attention to? Ignoring positive realities is a form of negative thinking.

- Sometimes there's no need to *change* anything. You may find that simply *observing* a negative thought or feeling dissolves it.

*Observation
is the key
to letting go.*

JOHN-ROGER

Fifty-nine:
Heal Thyself First

- As you learn more about yourself, you will also learn more about others. As you learn more about depression—and especially after the depression begins to lift—you'll probably notice a great many people you think need to be treated for *their* depression.

- One of the cleverest avoidances of treatment is to spend time "healing" others. Heal *yourself* first.

- The first few months of healing your depression is an important time. The more you participate in the treatment, the greater your healing will be. Recognizing negative habits, developing new skills, and learning to enjoy simply *being*—perhaps for the first time in your life—can be exhilarating *and* exhausting. Monitor your energy; reserve it for yourself.

- Is this being selfish? Sure. *Self*-ish. You're taking time for your*self*. Some might say that depression grows from an impoverished self; an inner being that has not been properly nourished. Nourish yourself. Become your own best gardener.*

- When you heal more fully, *that's* the time to reach out to others. You'll be able to help them far more from wholeness.

---

* Movie suggestion: rent the movie *Being There* and watch it while reflecting on being your own best gardener.

How can you say to your brother,
"Let me take the speck
out of your eye,"
when all the time
there is a plank in your own eye?
You hypocrite,
first take the plank
out of your own eye,
and then you will see clearly to
remove the speck
from your brother's eye.

JESUS OF NAZARETH

MATTHEW 7:4-5

Sixty:
No One or No Thing
Can Depress You
Unless You Allow It

- The buck stops here. More accurately, the *blame* stops here.

- You, and you alone, have the ability to depress yourself. "No one can make you feel inferior," wrote Eleanor Roosevelt, "without your consent."

- Short of directly *physically* harming you, all external events and people depress you because *you* think negative thoughts about them, *not because of what they do.*

- This is the foundation of personal responsibility: It's not what happens to you, but your *inner reaction* to what happens to you, that determines whether you feel miserable or marvelous.

- Using this *ability* to *respond* in a masterful way is response-ability.

- This idea, of course, brings on a chorus of, "Yes, but what about . . . ."

- People become *so involved* in creating outlandish scenarios in which another's actions *cause* them to feel bad. "Faced with the choice between changing one's mind and proving there is no need to do so," observed Professor John Kenneth Galbraith, "almost everyone gets busy on the proof."

Men are disturbed not by things,
but by the view
which they take of them.

EPICTETUS
FIRST CENTURY B.C.

- Rather than counter all the "Yes, buts . . ." individually, allow us to simply mention one name: Viktor Frankl, M.D. Dr. Frankl had *everything* and *everyone* in his life taken from him in, historically, the most appalling way possible. He is a survivor of the Holocaust. There's no need for detail here.

- What's important is the conclusion Dr. Frankl came to. While in the concentration camp, he realized one essential truth: no matter *what* they put him through, he still had within him the power to *choose* how he was going to order his inner environment—his thoughts, his feelings, his being.

- No matter how much they took from him—which was every person and material thing he had—he still had this freedom; this freedom to choose.*

- It's a freedom you have, too. You can't always choose what happens to you, but you can *always* choose your reaction to it. To react negatively to certain situations is not "just you." You may have bad habits that currently are "on automatic." But old habits can be broken; new habits can be learned.

- Becoming more responsible for your actions and feelings may seem like a lot of work. You're right. It *is* a lot of work.

- Freedom usually is.

---

* Dr. Frankl's book is entitled *Man's Search for Meaning.*

The last of
the human freedoms—
to choose one's attitude
in any given
set of circumstances;
to choose one's own way.

VIKTOR FRANKL, M.D.

Sixty-one:
"Yes" and "No"

- *Yes* and *no* are two invaluable words in obtaining and maintaining personal freedom. The secret? *Say the one you mean.*

- Yes and no guard your time. Think of them as the door of your house: the open door is yes, the closed door is no. If you open the door when you really want it closed, and close the door when you really want it open, you will soon find yourself with a house full of what you do not want. This is depressing, indeed.

- Too often, we say yes or no for the wrong reason. That reason, usually, is fear: we're afraid of a new experience; we're afraid of hurting someone's feelings; we're afraid someone might not like us; we're afraid of what other people might think, and so on.

- Yes and no are there to express what *you* want, what *your* preferences are, what *you* are willing to and not willing to do.

- Often, we're asked to say yes or no to a future event. How do we know *now* if we're going to want to do it *then*? A good indicator: If it were available to do *right now*, would you do it? Yes or no? When it comes time to do it, you'll be doing it "right now," because "then" has a sneaky way of becoming "now." So, if you don't want to do it now, you probably won't want to do it then.

I only have
"yes" men around me.
Who needs "no" men?

MAE WEST

Sixty-two:
It's Okay to Feel—Anything

- There are no "bad" feelings. Even "feeling bad" is not a "bad" feeling.

- The secret—whether up or down—is to enjoy the ride.

- Feel the full range of emotions available to you. People spend large amounts of time and money on movies, TV, videos, novels, and music so that they might *feel* something.

- Those who can make us feel the most, most often, are known as entertainment geniuses. We make them stars—and *rich*.

- Even if we don't respect *what* they create, we are still aware that it has the power to move us. ("Extraordinary," said Noel Coward, "how potent cheap music is.")

- There is such a thing as a healthy sadness— free from the self-pity and suffering of depression.

- Be *moved* by your own life. *Feel* it in all its fullness and glory.

The point is,
we are not rocks.
Who wants to be one anyway,
impermeable,
unchanging,
our history
already played out.

JOHN ROSENTHAL

Sixty-three:
Hurt, Resentment, and Guilt

- *Hurt, resentment,* and *guilt* are closely related. When something is taken away from us, or something we want is not made available to us, we can feel hurt. Hurt is difficult for people to feel and express. So, some people avoid it by turning to anger. If we get angry at someone or something *outside* ourselves, it's called resentment. If we get angry at *ourselves*, it's called guilt. Anytime you feel anger—whether it's expressed as guilt or resentment—there's hurt underneath it.

- If you catch the hurt early enough, you can move directly back to the *caring.* You're never hurt about anything you don't care about. *Switch* the caring from the disappointing object to another object about which you can "safely" care. (Here, having a love for God, nature, or the universe comes in handy.)

- If you don't catch the disappointment soon enough, you're left with hurt, guilt, and/or resentment. *Do something* with them—preferably something physical, but safe. A few deep breaths, a good stretch, walking, dancing, or singing. Silent screams, or noisy screams—if you can do them without frightening the horses. ("I don't care *what* they do," said Mrs. Patrick Campbell a century ago, "as long as they don't do it in the street and frighten the horses.") Cry, write down your negative thoughts and burn the paper. Lie on a bed and kick and scream. Beat a pil-

Burn from my brain
and from my breast
Sloth,
and the cowardice that clings,
And stiffness
and the soul's arrest:
And feed my brain
with better things.

G. K. CHESTERTON

low.

- If you seem to have a residue of hurt, resentment, or guilt, you might want to schedule a session with your therapist for some emotional "release" work.

- Notice that none of our suggestions for releasing negative feelings involves anyone other than you and a professional. We did not suggest, "Go and really tell them off. *Then* you'll feel better!" That seldom works. In the first place, people don't just stand there, as they do in the movies, and get told off. They tend to *interrupt*. (Well, you *knew* they were rude.) They usually start to tell *you* off. (The impertinence!) Finally, once they have been told off, they are *seldom* properly devastated. (How dare they?) And if they *act* devastated, how do you know they're not doing it just to make you feel guilty? (Those sneaky bastards!) "Peace of mind," wrote J. P. McEvoy, "is better than giving them 'a piece of your mind.'"

- *Communicating* your feelings with people you're close to is essential, but communication is not the same as venting, dumping, or telling off. In fact, it's often easier to communicate a negative feeling when you're *not* feeling it.

- Communicate hurt using "I" statements. ("I feel disappointed"; "I'm hurt when you don't call if you're going to be late"; "I'd prefer it if you would . . . .") And be sure to let them know that you only feel hurt because you *care*.

*In certain trying circumstances,
urgent circumstances,
desperate circumstances,
profanity furnishes a relief
denied even to prayer.*

MARK TWAIN

Sixty-four:
Forgiving

- Forgiving is a word that means just what it says: *for giving*. Whom are we for giving to? Those we forgive? Sometimes. Ourselves? *Always*. The primary reason to forgive is for *your* peace of mind, and the quality of all your future relationships. (For more on this, please see two of Harold's earlier books, *Making Peace with Yourself* and *Making Peace with Your Parents*.)

- Jesus of Nazareth was one of the greatest teachers of forgiveness. In the eye-for-an-eye, tooth-for-a-tooth world into which he came, forgiveness was a radical concept. (As it is today.) The word Jesus used for forgiveness meant to *let go*, to *untie*.

- That's what we do when we forgive: we *let go* of our imaginary (but painful) control of the way we think things *should* be, and we *untie* ourselves from the burden of judging the way they are. Forgiveness is a direct route to freedom, lightening up, and moving on.

- Forgiveness is a simple process: you say (aloud or to yourself), "I forgive . . ." then state the person (perhaps yourself), event, or occurrence you have judged. Then say, "I forgive myself for judging . . ." and state the same person, event, or occurrence. So, not only do you let go of the *judgment;* you let go of whatever judgment you've made *for having judged in the first place*. And then let the entire matter go.

- Forgive, forget, and move on with your life.

*Here is a mental treatment
guaranteed to cure every ill
that flesh is heir to:
sit for half an hour
every night and mentally
forgive everyone against whom
you have any ill will
or antipathy.*

CHARLES FILLMORE

Sixty-five:
Positive Distractions

- The *instant* you find yourself in a negative pattern, do something—anything—positive to break it. Take a deep breath, look out a window, smell a flower, eat an apple, drink some water, read a joke, sing a song, write a poem, say a prayer—the list is endless.

- It's sometimes difficult to "work through" a negative pattern while it's going on. So, interrupt it with a positive distraction.

- Make a list of your favorite positive distractions and memorize five that you can do practically anywhere. The next time you find yourself "stuck" in a negative pattern, immediately turn to one of your positive distractions. If one isn't distracting enough, try another, and another, and another.

- "The hardest thing you can do," wrote Allen Klein, "is smile when you are ill, in pain, or depressed. But this no-cost remedy is a necessary first step if you are to start on the road to recovery."

- Smile.

*Is there anything
men take more pains about
than to render themselves
unhappy?*

BENJAMIN FRANKLIN

Sixty-six:
Straighten up! Head up! Take a Deep Breath!

- The classic "depressed stance" is stooped over, head down, shoulders round. With such posture depressed people seem to be, as they say in *cliché*, "carrying the weight of the world on their shoulders."

- Consciously changing this posture can change the depressive mood. Head up, shoulders back, deep breath—and you tend to feel better.

- It's very hard to breathe deeply all slouched over, which can cut oxygen intake, which itself contributes to depression. Learn to breathe deeply, expanding your lower abdomen as you do.

- Experiment with different postures, ways of sitting, ways of walking, and so on, and see if some make you feel better than others.

This is my "depressed stance."
When you're depressed,
it makes a lot of difference
how you stand.
The worst thing you can do
is straighten up and
hold your head high
because then
you'll start to feel better.
If you're going to get any joy
out of being depressed,
you've got to stand like this.

CHARLIE BROWN

Sixty-seven:
Get Things Done
or Let Them Go

- Most people are overcommitted. There are so many books they plan to read, videotapes they plan to watch, dinners they plan to have, friends they plan to visit, closets they plan to clean (or come out of), classes they want to take, and on and on. If they added nothing to these "plans" and lived to be 302, they *still* wouldn't get them all done.

- This backlog of "I've-been-meaning-to," can be depressing.

- This is especially true when the things we mean to do are *important*—charitable works, exercise programs for health, quality time with loved ones, religious or spiritual practices, political causes, social change, and the like. Here, not only do we miss the satisfaction and enjoyment of doing them, we also feel guilty for not having done them.

- There are two ways to effectively deal with such past commitments: do them, or be done with them. Get them done, or let them go.

- To break the cycle of depression, reprioritize and then *move*. Get those things done. Accomplish them.

- Or, declare to yourself that you are no longer going to do them—at least not at this time. (Be reasonable about this—if you owe someone money, for example, you can't just "declare" it paid.) It's not that what you want to do is no

*Life is too short
to stuff a mushroom.*

STORM JAMESON

longer important to you; it's just that your resources are otherwise engaged. "I can't do this," is seldom true. "I'd like to do this, but my resources are otherwise engaged," more often is.

- It's a good idea to make a list of all the things you said, either to yourself or to others, you were going to do. (The listing of the things you said to yourself will probably be considerably longer than the list of commitments you made to others.) Then check off the ones associated with essentials (food, shelter, healing your depression) and notice how much time you have left for all the rest. Start checking off, one by one, what you still have time and resources to do.

- At some point, as happens to us all, you will run out of time and resources.

- Then, *cross off* the rest. As you cross each item off, say, "Yes, I'd like to do this, but my resources are otherwise engaged. For now, I declare it done." (When communicating with others, it's probably a good idea to leave off the "I declare it done" part.)

- In doing this, you'll probably notice an increase in energy, a clarity of mind, and a stronger desire to get done those things you really *do* plan on doing.

- And (need we point out?) be *very* watchful in making future commitments—to others, and *especially* to yourself.

Before I was married
I was courting my wife
ten years.
Then I went round
to see her father.
And I looked straight at him.
He said, "Hello."
I said, "Hello."
He said, "What do you want?"
I said, "I've been courting
your daughter for ten years."
He said, "So?"
I said, "I want to marry her."
He said, "I thought you
wanted a pension."

MAX MILLER

Sixty-eight:
Affirmations and
Visualizations

- An *affirm*ation is to make something *firm*. We take something as ephemeral as a thought and make it firm—that is, *real*—in the physical world. (Reading this book began as a thought in your mind—an affirmation—and you repeated that thought often enough that it has now become a physical reality: you are reading this book.)

- To *visualize* is to see the affirmation taking place in your imagination.

- Don't be misled by the word *visual:* many people don't "see" a picture in their imagination—for some it's more *feeling;* for others it's more *hearing.* Remember what a triangle looks like? A red apple? The Statue of Liberty? That's what your visualization is like. The way we remember the past is the way we "see" the future.

- We use affirmations and visualizations all the time. It's how we human beings create.

- Our thoughts—which include our imagination—create emotions, biological reactions, physical actions, and we use these to gather to us people and things.

- Almost everyone uses the process of affirmation and visualization—usually unconsciously—in both positive and negative ways. We are, of course, suggesting that you use them in more positive ways.

When there is no vision,
the people perish.

PROVERBS 29:18

- When people refer to affirmations and visualizations, they almost always mean *positive* affirmations and visualizations.

- Affirmations are simply statements of what you want to be, do, and have. They are best stated in the present, as though you were already being, doing, and having them. Affirmations, then, usually begin with, "I am . . . ." "I am joyful and happy," "I am loving my life," "I am contented and grateful in this moment."

- This naturally leads you into visualizations—imagining yourself in happy and joyful situations, loving various aspects of your life, being contented and grateful in this moment.

- Make a list of positive affirmations. Say them over and over, anywhere you are. Write them on cards and place the cards around as reminders: on the dashboard of your car, the mirror where you dress, the ceiling above your bed. Visualize what your life would be like if these affirmations were true.

- Keep affirming and keep visualizing, and they *will* be true. As Maharishi Mahesh Yogi explained, "That which we give attention to grows stronger in our lives."

*Visualize yourself as sound,
healthy and filled with
the vitality and boundless life
of your Creator.
Look upon yourself as
the unique individual
that you are.
Get in harmony
with the creative,
life-giving,
health-maintaining
forces of the universe.
Affirm peace,
wholeness,
and good health—
and they will be yours.*

NORMAN VINCENT PEALE

Sixty-nine:
Light and Meditation

- *Light* is a concept that has permeated religious, spiritual, philosophical, and even scientific beliefs throughout history, from ancient civilizations to advanced quantum physics.

- You may consider light as the light of God, the light of the Holy Spirit, the light of nature, the light of the sun, the light within us all, or the electromagnetic waves of energy that physicists tell us make up the entire known universe, visible and invisible, including the book you're holding, the light reflecting off the page that allows you to read the book, your hands that are holding the book, your eyes that are perceiving the reflected-light images, and your brain that is making sense of the whole thing; these, or any other concept of light you may have, are fine with us. (Who says we don't know how to write long sentences?)

- Let us simply define light as *the invisible message of goodness from the Divine.*

- You can use the light to surround, fill, and heal yourself. You can send it ahead, or send it anywhere you like—even forward or backwards in time. You can breathe deeply of the light. Whenever you use or send the light, it's a good idea to ask for it to go "for the highest good of all concerned." Don't use the light as a form of control. Let it be used as an affirmation of the statement, "Thy will be done."

- As depression is so often associated with

*I have discovered that
all man's unhappiness
derives from only one source—
not being able to
sit quietly in a room.*

PASCAL

1670

darkness, asking those dark parts of your life—both inside and outside yourself—to be filled with light can be profoundly uplifting.

- A good way of doing this is through *meditation*. During meditation, we can ask that any dark, heavy aspects of our lives—past, present, or future—be filled with light. We can imagine the darkness dissolving and the heaviness lightening.

- Sometimes in meditation, we just want to listen—listen to ourselves, or to whatever or whomever we consider to be a source of Divine inspiration. ("Prayer is when you talk to God," as John-Roger once said. "Meditation is when you let God talk to you.") Sometimes it's fun just to sit and listen to the mind chattering on.

- Meditation can be used to contemplate an idea, thought, or even a physical object that you consider meaningful, profound, or beautiful. When you hear something nice and tell yourself, "I'll have to think about that," meditation is a good time to think about it.

- There are so many forms of meditation (including the Transcendental Meditation Technique, which Harold has used and recommends highly), taught in so many ways: books, tapes, classes. It's a rich world to explore.

- Meditation is a time you can spend with yourself, as well as your *self.*

*Sadness flies
on the wings of the morning
and out of the heart of darkness
comes the light.*

JEAN GIRAUDOUX

Seventy:
Lighten Up—Life Is Funnier Than We Thought

- Laughter is an amazingly rapid healer of depression. So is humor. Humor doesn't necessarily make you laugh, but it does make you smile inside.

- We're going to step aside now to hear from the experts:

  This I conceive to be the chemical function of humor: to change the character of our thought. —**Lin Yutang**

  Laughter lets me relax. It's the equivalent of taking a deep breath, letting it out, and saying, "This too will pass." —**Odette Pollar**

  Not a shred of evidence occurs in favor of the idea that life is serious. —**Brendan Gill**

  Warning: Humor may be hazardous to your illness. —**Ellie Katz**

  Happiness is no laughing matter. —**Archbishop Whately of Dublin (1787–1863)**

  I'm all for rational enjoyment, and so forth, but I think a fellow makes himself conspicuous when he throws soft-boiled eggs at the electric fan. —**P. G. Wodehouse**

  We are all here for a spell, get all the good laughs you can. —**Will Rogers**

- Rent funny movies, buy funny cassettes, read funny books, watch funny shows. Observe your life.

- Doctor's orders!

Laughter, n.
An interior convulsion,
producing a distortion
of the features and accompanied
by inarticulate noises.
It is infectious and,
though intermittent,
incurable.

AMBROSE BIERCE

Seventy-one:
Music

- If, as William Congreve observed in 1697, "Music has charms to soothe a savage breast, To soften rocks, or to bend a knotted oak," surely, then, it also has the charms to soothe and soften a savage depression.

- Music you find soothing can make an excellent addition to meditation, or it can be a meditation in itself. Whether it's the second movement of Beethoven's *Third Concerto for Piano and Orchestra*, or the first twelve hours of Mantovani's *Four-hundred-and-sixty-seventh Concerto for Elevator and Supermarket*, whatever music you find soothing, put it on, close your eyes, and drift away.

- Of course, music does more than just soothe; it can stimulate or enhance almost any activity, emotion, or mood—from crying, to dancing, to mystical visions. Music—carefully selected—is a way to elicit suppressed feelings in need of expression and catharsis.

- The idea is not just to have background music, but to spend some time with it; focus on it; relax into it. "Music heard so deeply," wrote T. S. Eliot, "That it is not heard at all, but you are the music / While the music lasts."

- Thanks to today's technology, the music can last and last.

We are a spectacular,
splendid manifestation of life.
We have language.
We have affection.
We have genes for usefulness,
and usefulness is about as close
to a "common goal" of nature
as I can guess at.
And finally,
and perhaps best of all,
we have music.

LEWIS THOMAS

Seventy-two:
The Opposite of Depression Is Expression

- What playful, creative things do you do—or have wanted to do? Paint? Write? Sew? Dance? Cook? Garden? Sing? Act? Compose? Play (an instrument, a game, a sport)?

- Well, *do it!*

- Don't worry about being good at it, or making a living at it, or even sharing it with anybody. *Just have fun with it.* Let yourself *play*.

- We forget about play, we adults—especially we depressed adults. It's a contributing factor to depression. Too often, even when we're having fun, we do it passively—watching a movie, watching TV, watching sports. This is fine, but we're suggesting you also do something that gets you *actively involved*.

- As the ultimate expert on life, Ward Cleaver, once put it: "You're never too old to do goofy stuff."

When you're depressed,
the whole body is depressed,
and it translates
to the cellular level.
The first objective is
to get your energy up,
and you can do it through play.
It's one of the most powerful
ways of breaking up hopelessness
and bringing energy
into the situation.

O. CARL SIMONTON, M.D.

Seventy-three:
Gratitude

- We have *so much* to be grateful for, and yet depression robs us of gratitude. Or is it that, perhaps, we fall into the painful habit of ingratitude, and depression results? One of the nicest ways out of depression is to have frequent gratitude breaks.

- As Randall Miller pointed out, "You can't be depressed and grateful at the same time."

- Look around. Be grateful for what's around you. Actually say to yourself, "I am grateful for the lamp. I am grateful for my hands. I am grateful for the couch . . . ." Let yourself feel a little gratitude before moving on to the next object. Don't forget to be grateful if you can see, hear, touch, taste, smell.

- Run out of things to be grateful for? Okay, try this: breathe out all your air. Hold it. You'll be *very* grateful for a breath of air shortly.

- Share your gratitude with others: "That was beautiful," "You look lovely," "I appreciate what you did for me." There is no need for gushing sentimentality or false flattery. The goal is to express appreciation freely and appropriately.

- In any moment, there's something to be grateful for. That we don't spontaneously focus on the good is merely a bad habit. Learn a new habit, a better habit: focus on the positive. More and more, you will have that *great*, *full* feeling.

Love your eyes that can see,
your mind that can
Hear the music,
the thunder of the wings.
Love the wild swan.

ROBINSON JEFFERS

My grandfather always said
that living
is like licking honey
off a thorn.

LOUIS ADAMIC

Part IV
As Healing Continues ...

This last part of the book offers some thoughts, suggestions, and encouragements; things to do, consider, and enjoy, as your healing continues.

Seventy-four:
Your Healing
Has Already Begun

- Some people will read all the way through this book before seeking a professional consultation to evaluate depression. Other people, who are reading this book on the recommendation of their doctor or therapist, may already be well into treatment.

- Wherever you are in the treatment process, know that your healing has already begun.

- Healing begins as an inner decision. *Any* physical action that supports that decision indicates healing is underway.

- Just picking up a book entitled *How to Heal Depression* and reading this far in it shows that your healing has begun.

- Never before has the quest to heal depression been so swiftly and abundantly rewarded.

- Once treatment begins, you are very likely to wonder, "Where has *this* been all my life?" The truth is, it hasn't been *available* for most of your life.

- Congratulations on your courage to heal.

*It isn't for
the moment you are stuck
that you need courage,
but for the long uphill climb
back to sanity and security.*

ANNE MORROW LINDBERG

Seventy-five:
Patience

- When being treated for a medical condition, we become the patient.

- We also suggest that you treat yourself well by *becoming patient*.

- As we previously discussed, antidepressant medication can often take weeks to work. Sometimes it takes months to discover the best antidepressant for you and to arrive at the ideal dosage. Looking *back* on this time from a nondepressed state, the healing seems miraculously swift. Looking *ahead*, to the possibility of more weeks of depression, this period can seem to be a long time indeed.

- Give yourself time. Give your health practitioners time. Give nature time.

- Be patient with your impatience.

- If patience is too much to ask, at least *endure*. Hang in there. Hold on. Stick with it. Healing is on its way.

*Patience, and the mulberry leaf
becomes a silk gown.*

CHINESE PROVERB

Seventy-six:
Think Big, but Not Huge

- As you envision your healing, hold a vision of what you'd like the "healed you" to be. Words such as *contentment, well-being, enthusiasm, joyful, happy, effective, loving, tender,* and others may come to mind.

- When dreaming of your healing, it's fine to think big.

- But don't think *too* big. *Never* being angry, sad, hurt, disappointed, or feeling any other emotion you associate with depression is not a reasonable goal. Strive for excellence, not perfection.

- Yes, as you heal from depression, the general shift of emotions—mood, if you will—should definitely be on the upswing. *Never, ever* feeling bad again is not, well, *human*.

- Your psychiatrist or therapist can help you set reasonable personal goals as you heal.

We are not human beings
having a spiritual experience.
We are spiritual beings
having a human experience.

PIERRE TEILHARD DE CHARDIN

Seventy-seven:
Healing Has Its
Ups and Downs

- Healing from depression—or healing from anything else, for that matter—is not a smooth, even, steady, upward path. It tends to look more like this:

- It's like a roller coaster, a *slow* roller coaster for the most part, one that lets you off at a higher point than where you got on.

- Ride the ride. Follow your treatment. Soon you'll find that the downs of today were the ups of yesterday.

*If only we'd stop
trying to be happy
we could have
a pretty good time.*

EDITH WHARTON

Seventy-eight:
Seek the Support of Others

- For you it's a time for change, for growth, for healing. Change can sometimes seem chaotic, confusing, frightening. Seek the support of others.

- Ask trusted friends or family members to help with specific tasks or ongoing responsibilities.

- Although, as we mentioned, it's a good idea to postpone major decisions, if decisions must be made, ask for the opinions of others you respect in making your choice.

- Ask people who have been through treatment for depression and are further along in the healing process to be available for phone calls, questions, or chats. Sometimes nothing is so reassuring as a simple, "Oh, yeah, I went through that."

- Ask your boss if it's possible to have your workload lightened for a while.

- Ask if certain commitments might be put off until later.

- People may say no—but at least give them a chance to say yes.

True happiness
is of a retired nature,
and an enemy
to pomp and noise;
it arises, in the first place,
from the enjoyment of one's self,
and, in the next,
from the friendship
and conversation of
a few select companions.

JOSEPH ADDISON

1712

Seventy-nine:
Support Groups

- People often benefit by gathering with others going through similar experiences. Those who are healing from depression are no exception.

- Often these groups form around the principles of Cognitive/Interpersonal Therapy, or are made up of people who are taking antidepressant medications, or both.

- Support groups are an excellent place to share experiences, suggestions, information, and, as the title of the group indicates, *support*.

- Perhaps the most important knowledge to be gained from support groups is *you are not alone*. (Now where have we heard *that* phrase before?) You might discover, for example, that a problem you thought was yours and yours alone, is so common that the group has given it a number. ("Right! That's number 43.") Or, someone may share an experience that sounds interesting, but you can't quite relate to it. A week later, it happens to you.

- Your psychiatrist, doctor, or therapist may be able to recommend support groups in your area.

- A support group is made up of human beings who care about and are committed to their own healing. By self-selection alone, then, support groups are populated by supportive, wonderful people.

*Adversity is the state
in which a man most easily
becomes acquainted with himself,
being especially
free from admirers then.*

DR. SAMUEL JOHNSON

Eighty:
Twelve-Step and Recovery Programs

- The most successful treatment ever created for addiction is the Twelve-Step Program of Alcoholics Anonymous. It has been adapted and used successfully in treating just about every addiction, bad habit, or emotional problem in the human sphere.

- The secret of the Twelve-Step Program is that it is, in reality, important rules for personal growth. Following these steps leads to greater personal maturity, integrity, and freedom.

- This upward growth gives the inner strength to focus on something other than the addiction.

- While depression is not an addiction, people with depression often become addicted to other things, from food to sex to drugs to smoking to procrastination to alcohol to negative thinking.* In overcoming any of these, Twelve-Step Programs can be valuable.

---

* An excellent book on overcoming the addiction to negative thinking is *You Can't Afford the Luxury of a Negative Thought*, by John-Roger and Peter McWilliams.

THE TWELVE STEPS

1. We admitted we were powerless over our addiction—that our lives had become unmanageable.

2. Came to believe that a Power greater than ourselves could restore us to sanity.

3. Made a decision to turn our will and our lives over to the care of this Higher Power, as we understood Him, Her, or It.

4. Made a searching and fearless moral inventory of ourselves.

5. Admitted to our Higher Power, to ourselves, and to another human being the exact nature of our wrongs.

6. Were entirely ready to have our Higher Power remove all these defects of character.

7. Humbly asked our Higher Power to remove our shortcomings.

8. Made a list of all persons we had harmed, and became willing to make amends to them all.

9. Made direct amends to such people wherever possible, except when to do so would injure them or others.

10. Continued to take personal inventory and when we were wrong, promptly admitted it.

11. Sought, through prayer and meditation, to improve our conscious contact with our Higher Power as we understood Him, Her, or It, praying only for knowledge of our Higher Power's will for us and the power to carry that out.

12. Having had a spiritual awakening as the result of these steps, we tried to carry this message to others and to practice these principles in all our affairs.

Eighty-one:
Praise Yourself

- It takes courage to accept the possibility that you might have a depressive illness.

- It's courageous to make a medical appointment for a diagnostic evaluation.

- It's courageous to enter onto a course of treatment that is frightening to some and ridiculed by others.

- It takes wisdom and courage to work with your psychiatrist or doctor to find the right medication, and with your therapist on deeply personal and challenging issues.

- Praise yourself for all this. Praise yourself for every little victory, every step taken on the path of healing—including those that don't work. It's all part of the journey.

- Keep reminding yourself that who you really are is much more than your depression.

- Praise yourself for your courage to learn, risk, and grow.

- Well done!

Life is made up
of small pleasures.
Happiness is made up
of those tiny successes.
The big ones
come too infrequently.
And if you don't collect
all these tiny successes
the big ones
don't really mean anything.

NORMAN LEAR

Eighty-two:
Give Yourself Time to Heal

- Healing takes time. Even if you—like so many people who begin treatment for depression—find marked improvement in just a few weeks, the complete process of healing may take longer.

- The longer you've been depressed, the longer the body is likely to need to heal. Give it the time it needs. If you, like many people with long-term, low-grade depression, can't even *remember* when you weren't depressed, relax: you're now healing from the ravages of a lifetime.

- Fortunately, as you heal, time passes more enjoyably. *Just sitting* can be enjoyable. In fact, one moves more and more into "the moment," or the "here and now" that saints, both eastern and western, have described. (Some even claim enjoying the moment is the goal of life.)

- The more you heal, the less you're concerned about whether your healing is "done"— a sure sign that you're healing.

*It does not matter
how slowly you go
so long as you do not stop.*

CONFUCIUS

Eighty-three:
Be Gentle with Yourself

- Just as you asked others for support, ask *yourself* for support.

- Be gentle with yourself, be easy, give yourself a break. A major symptom of depression is being hard on yourself. Soften up; lighten up. Remember that mistakes are something "this flesh is heir to."

- The next time you want to attack yourself, have a laugh attack instead. Consider how silly it is to be at war with yourself.

- Imagine two armies facing each other in the trenches. One soldier looks up from one side, another soldier looks up from the other—and they have the same face. They begin pointing and laughing hysterically. Other soldiers cautiously peek out of trenches and around barricades, only to discover their mirror images cautiously peeking back at them. All the faces are yours. The entire battlefield dissolves in waves of laughter. End of war. Beginning of Monty Python sketch.

- And now, here's one of the most radical thoughts you will ever read: *it's okay to feel good when things go bad.*

Compassion for myself
is the most powerful
healer of them all.

THEODORE ISAAC RUBIN, M.D.

Eighty-four:
View Problems As Creative Challenges

- During depression, it's easy to view problems as burdens, interruptions, something else to struggle through—in short, *upsetting*.

- As the depression lifts, it's easier to see problems as creative challenges, invitations to activity, even *games*.

- *Problems do not need to make you unhappy.*

- Think of life as a *process* to be enjoyed *as you go along.*

- Too often depressive thinking says, "When I get through this, *then* I'll be happy." With that thinking, it's no wonder one is seldom—if ever—happy. Did you ever notice that problems just "keep on comin'"?

- So, when a problem arises, view it with the attitude you'd have if your best friends said, "Let's play Monopoly (or poker, or canasta, or touch football, or whatever your favorite game is).

- Enthusiasm, creativity, playfulness, and a bemused sense of humor are the keys.

More damn fun!

JOHN MORTON

Eighty-five:
Seek Comforting

- Being hugged, stroked, nurtured, and adored is a perfectly natural desire. When the need arises, do what you can to fulfill it.

- A professional massage—or a series of them—is an excellent investment in healing.

- Perhaps the comforting comes not by touch, but by touch tone. Make a list of friends, support group members, relatives, and others whom you can call and say, "Tell me I'm okay!"

*A person will be
called to account
on Judgment Day
for every permissible thing
he might have enjoyed
but did not.*

TALMUD

Eighty-six:
Relationships May Change

- As you heal, you may find your relationships change.

- The relationships based on the "depressed you" tend to wither, while the relationships with people who like you for the *real* you often grow stronger.

- Treatment for depression does not make people "the same." Far from it. As depression lifts, the individual qualities of the person tend to surface and are naturally expressed. One may even develop an eccentricity or two. This deeply upsets those who count on you to be your "old, predictable self."

- Some people prey upon the weaknesses of depressed people, using fear, guilt, and unworthiness to manipulate and control. As these symptoms of depression heal, you become less needy, less manipulatable.

- This, obviously, does not please the controllers or manipulators. They may try to manipulate you out of treatment. Don't let them.

- Don't make any firm decisions about relationships until your healing is well underway. Observe what's happening inside yourself and with others. There's time to make choices later.

- But beware: if you fail to attend one of the regularly scheduled meetings of the Ain't-It-Awful Club, guess who gets talked about?

- Ain't it awful?

To laugh often and love much,
to win the respect
of intelligent persons
and the affection of children;
to earn the approbation
of honest critics;
to appreciate beauty;
to give of one's self;
to know even one life
has breathed easier
because you have lived—
that is to have succeeded.

HARRY EMERSON FOSDICK

Eighty-seven:
Enjoy the Good

- Don't be surprised if good things happen to you *without your even trying*.

- Struggle, effort, and trying are, for many depressed people, the only way they know to get something good.

- As depression heals, good things tend to happen—spontaneously. Accept them. Enjoy them.

- You may, for example, find yourself simply not wanting to continue a bad habit you thought would take enormous effort to overcome. Or, you may find yourself naturally wanting to take part in a healthy activity that you figured would require tremendous discipline.

- You may find career opportunities, relationships, and even your health becoming more of what you want them to be—simply because you are *being* more of who you *are*.

- "Enjoy life," the bumper sticker reminds us. "This is not a rehearsal."

*What a
wonderful life I've had!
I only wish
I'd realized it sooner.*

COLETTE

Eighty-eight: Making Peace with Depression

- Clinical research indicates that approximately:

    —One-third of the people who are treated for depression heal completely. They never need antidepressant medications or treatment again.

    —One-third of the people heal completely and are taken off antidepressant medication. Later, however, a depression returns and it must be treated again, usually with antidepressants.

    —One-third of the people will need antidepressant medication on a long-term basis.

- There's no way of telling which path your depression will take. The important thing is that the depression can be contained and the symptoms eliminated—as in the treatment of high blood pressure, low thyroid, or diabetes.

- The point is that either one heals oneself from depression; one heals oneself from depression and it returns (in which case it can be successfully treated again); or depression is a fact of life (for which, ongoing, long-term treatment can be safe and successful with periodic medical supervision.)

- So, make peace with depression. It's not an enemy. It's not out to "get ya." It's just an

*Riches are not from
an abundance of worldly goods,
but from a contented mind.*

MOHAMMED

imbalance of the biochemistry of the brain and/or the thought patterns of the mind. As with any illness, it needs ongoing acceptance and healing.

We should be taught
not to wait for
inspiration to start
a thing.
Action always
generates inspiration.
Inspiration seldom
generates action.

FRANK TIBOLT

Eighty-nine:
Society and Depression
(the Good News)

- Imagine for a moment that the millions and millions of depressed people in this country were no longer depressed:

    —They no longer blame themselves or others for the symptoms of an illness.

    —They have more energy, get angry less quickly, are less prone to physical illness, and are free from addictions.

    —They laugh more and care more about themselves and their fellow human beings.

    —They are more productive, tolerant, giving, and forgiving.

- Whether this sounds like Sir Thomas More's *Utopia*, Louis Armstrong's "What a Wonderful World," or John Lennon's "Imagine," it does describe what is possible—for the first time in human history.

- Take an extreme case: the homeless. Have you ever spoken with a homeless person who you would say *wasn't* clinically depressed? Well, neither have we. Whether they're depressed because they're homeless or they're homeless because they're depressed no longer matters—treat the depression and perhaps a good number of the homeless will become productive citizens again.

- Healthy individuals make healthy societies.

*If one only wished to be happy,
this could be easily accomplished;
but we wish to be
happier than other people,
and this is always difficult,
for we believe others to be
happier than they are.*

MONTESQUIEU

Ninety:
Society and Depression
(the Bad News)

- It is estimated that untreated depression costs this country 43.7 *billion dollars* per year.

- With so much undiagnosed, misdiagnosed, untreated, and undertreated depression in this country, what are we, as a country, doing about it? Not much.

- Yes, the National Institutes of Health is doing a good job educating the American public about depression and its treatment. But it's not enough.

- Medicaid and Medicare will *not* pay for the latest generation of antidepressants (Prozac, Paxil, Zoloft, Effexor). Treatment with these drugs costs about five dollars a day—which is not a problem for a middle to upper-middle class person—but it can be devastating to a lower income person whose *food* budget is less than five dollars a day.

- This lack of healthcare coverage is especially distressing because it is estimated that as many as *sixty-five percent* of the elderly in this country have a clinical depression. A good number of the elderly depend on Medicare for their medical treatment.

- What if one of the reasons people are trapped in poverty is depression? What if giving them proper treatment allowed them to work their way *out* of poverty?

*How come dumb stuff
seems so smart
while you're doing it?*

DENNIS THE MENACE

- Do our elderly and lower income citizens deserve such *lack* of treatment?

- Equally startling is how economically wasteful this policy is. Many people are being treated for specific *symptoms* of depression at a great cost (for sleeping pills, sedatives, pain pills, etc.), when five dollars' worth of antidepressants would, by treating the depression, relieve most of the symptoms.

- Why waste money ineffectively treating *symptoms*?

- These are questions the government somehow has not fully considered. If you have any thoughts on this matter, please drop a note to your elected officials.

- When you hear depressing news, there's no point becoming depressed *about* it. Either do something about it, or determine that someone else is going to do something about it, and then let it go.

Concern should
drive us into action
and not into a depression.

KAREN HORNEY

Ninety-one:
Giving to Others

- Someone once asked: "If you were arrested for kindness, would there be enough evidence to convict you?" It's an interesting question. The answers are often more interesting.

- As your treatment reaches its conclusion, and as your healing continues, you may find that your healing is enhanced by giving to others.

- What do we give to others? We give of what we have. Among the things *you* have is the knowledge that (a) depression is an illness, and (b) depression is a *treatable* illness.

- A lot of people—roughly ten million in the United States alone—are waiting for that information.

- To the degree you can, and in the ways you know how, give them that information. We wrote a book. That's what we knew how to do. If you feel so moved, do what you can.

- No, we are not asking you to become the local proselytizer of antidepressants. We're simply saying that if there's one person who might be inspired by your story, consider telling it.

- Then let the person decide how, when, and if he or she will use the information you so kindly supplied.

Lighting your own light,
letting your own beacon shine,
this will then inspire others
who will inspire others
who will inspire others.

LAZARIS

Ninety-two:
Thank You and
Enjoy Your Journey

- Thank you for reading our book. Glance through it again and again as you move along your path of healing.

- In closing, we want you to know that we have walked this road ahead of you. We have deep compassion for all depressed people go through because we, too, have suffered from depression.

- We also know how difficult it was to read the writing on the wall (even though it was written in neon letters twelve feet high), to seek treatment, and to "hang in there" until the treatment was successful.

- So, we are not just authors and you are not just readers: we are all human beings—magnificent and monstrous, phenomenal and foolish, grasping selfishly and giving unconditionally.

- And you know what? We wouldn't have it any other way.

- Thanks for joining us.

- Enjoy your journey!

It's been troubling me.
Now, why is it that most of us
can talk openly about
the illnesses of our bodies,
but when it comes to our brain
and illnesses of the mind
we clam up
and because we clam up,
people with emotional disorders
feel ashamed,
stigmatized
and don't seek the help
that can make the difference.

KIRK DOUGLAS

*Suffering isn't ennobling,
recovery is.*

CHRISTIAAN N. BARNARD, M.D.

Recommended Reading on Depression

- *You Mean I Don't Have To Feel This Way? New Help For Depression, Anxiety and Addiction*, Collette Dowling.

- *Overcoming Depression*, Demitri Papolos, M.D. and Janice Papolos.

- *When the Blues Won't Go Away, New Approaches to Dysthymic Disorder and Other Forms of Chronic Low Grade Depression*, Robert M.A. Hirschfeld, MD; with S. Meltsner.

- *Feeling Good*, David D. Burns, M.D.; preface by Aaron T. Beck, M.D.

- *Interpersonal Psychotherapy of Depression*, Gerald L. Klerman, M.D.; Myrna M. Weissman, PhD; Bruce J. Rounsaville, M.D.; Eve S. Chevron, M.S.

- *From Sad to Glad*, Nathan S. Kline, M.D.

- *Moodswing*, Ronald R. Fieve, M.D.

- *Darkness Visible, A Memoir of Madness*, William Styron.

- *A Brilliant Madness, Living With Manic-Depressive Illness*, Patty Duke and Gloria Hockman.

All titles, and a catalog of other books, available from:

National Depressive and
Manic-Depressive Association
730 N. Franklin, Suite 501,
Chicago, IL 60610
(312) 642–0049
(312) 642–7243 FAX.

About the Authors

 **HAROLD H. BLOOMFIELD, M.D.,** is one of the leading psychological educators of our time. A Yale-trained psychiatrist, Dr. Bloomfield is an adjunct professor of psychology at Union Graduate School. From his first book, *TM*, which was a major international bestseller on the *New York Times* list for over six months, to his recent bestseller, *How to Survive the Loss of a Love*, which has sold over two million books, Dr. Bloomfield has been at the forefront of many important self-help movements worldwide. His other bestsellers, *Making Peace with Your Parents and Making Peace with Yourself*, introduced personal and family peacemaking to millions of people. Dr. Bloomfield's books have sold over five million copies and have been translated into twenty-two languages. His newest books are *Love Secrets for a Lasting Relationship, Making Peace in Your Stepfamily, How to Heal Depression*, and *Power of 5*.

Dr. Bloomfield is a frequent guest on "The Oprah Winfrey Show," "Donahue," "Sally Jessy Raphael," "Larry King Live," "Good Morning America," and CNN and ABC news specials. In addition to professional journals, his work and popular articles appear in *USA Today, Los Angeles Times, San Francisco Examiner, Cosmopolitan, Ladies' Home Journal, New Woman*, and *American Health*.

Dr. Bloomfield has received of the *Medical Self-Care* Magazine Book of the Year Award, the Golden Apple Award for Outstanding Psychological Educator, and the American Holistic Health Association's Lifetime Achievement Award. He is a member of the American Psychiatric Association and the San Diego Psychiatric Society.

Dr. Bloomfield maintains a private practice of psychiatry, psychotherapy, executive counseling, and family business consulting in Del Mar, California.

Dr. Bloomfield is a much admired keynote speaker for public programs, corporate meetings, and professional conferences. For further information regarding personal appearances, lectures, and seminars, please contact:

Harold H. Bloomfield, M.D., 1049 Camino Del Mar, Del Mar, California 92014   Office: 619–481–9950   FAX: 619–792–2333

PETER MCWILLIAMS has been writing about his passions since 1967. In that year, he became passionate about what most seventeen-year-olds are passionate about—love—and wrote *Come Love With Me & Be My Life*. This began a series of poetry books which have sold nearly four million copies.

Along with love, of course, comes loss, so Peter became passionate about emotional survival. In 1971 he wrote *Surviving the Loss of a Love*, which was expanded in 1976 and again in 1991 (with co-authors Melba Colgrove, Ph.D., and Harold Bloomfield, M.D.) into *How to Survive the Loss of a Love*. It has sold more than two million copies.

His passion for computers (or more accurately, for what computers can do) led to *The Personal Computer Book*, which *Time* proclaimed "a beacon of simplicity, sanity and humor," and the *Wall Street Journal* called "genuinely funny." (Now, really, how many people has the *Wall Street Journal* called "genuinely funny"?)

His passion for personal growth continues in the ongoing LIFE 101 Series with co-author John-Roger. Thus far, the books in this series are *You Can't Afford the Luxury of a Negative Thought*, *LIFE 101 (a New York Times* bestseller in both hardcover and paperback), *DO IT! (a #1 New York Times* hardcover bestseller), *WEALTH 101*, and *We Give To Love*.

His passion for visual beauty led him to publish, in 1992, his first book of photography, *PORTRAITS*, a twenty-two-year anthology of his photographic work.

Personal freedom, individual expression, and the right to live one's own life, as long as one does not harm the person or property of another, have long been his passions. His book, *Ain't Nobody's Business If You Do: The Absurdity of Consensual Crimes in a Free Society*, speaks of this passion.

Peter McWilliams has appeared on "The Oprah Winfrey Show," "Larry King" (both radio and television), "Donahue," "Sally Jessy Raphael," and "Talk Soup."

Acknowledgements (Harold)

I wish to praise the researchers who developed the breakthrough medical and psychological treatments of depression, including Aaron Beck, John Feighner, Ronald Fieve, Mark Gold, Gerald Klerman, Nathan Kline, Solomon Snyder, and Myrna Weissman.

I want to give gratitude to all my teachers, especially Lazaris and Maharishi Mahesh Yogi.

Special thanks to those whom it has been my privilege to serve as a psychiatrist and psychotherapist.

My heartfelt appreciation to Robert and Leslie Cooper, Mike and Donna Fletcher, John and Bonnie Gray, Susanna Gomez (my devoted personal assistant), Patricia Hayes, Christopher Hills, Hoffman Quadrinity Process Teachers Barbara Comstock and Carolyne Johnson, Noel Johansen, Robert and Phyllis Kory, Arnold Lazarus, Norman and Lyn Lear, Marly Meadows (my wonderful office manager), Vince and Laura Regalbuto, Ayman and Rowan Sawaf, Ted and Diana Wentworth, and my dear sister Nora and her husband Gus Stern.

My love and admiration for my dear parents, Fridl and Max.

My love and gratitude to my beloved wife, Sirah Vettese, for her devotion and contributions to this book. (FROM PETER: Thanks, Sirah!)

Much love and appreciation to my daughter Shazara and my stepsons, Michael and Damien, for their patience, understanding, and support.

*The purpose of life
is the expansion
of happiness.*

MAHARISHI MAHESH YOGI

Acknowledgement (Peter)

I have only one acknowledgement for this book, and that's Harold. For more than a year he dropped friendly hints that *maybe just perhaps* a few of my well-analyzed, well-explored, well-documented problems *might just* be due to a depression.

The only things larger than my depression, as it turns out, were my denial (which was *so* logical and *so* eloquent) and my ego (which was quite certain I could handle it on my own any time I wanted to—all I had to do was *apply* myself a little more).

It took more than a year for me to work out my prejudices and ignorances concerning depression ("Mental illness!"), antidepressant medications ("Drugs!"), and all the rest. Looking back, my concerns seem so silly. At the time, of course, they were as real as my misery.

Here I am, months after treatment (expertly and lovingly administered by Dr. B, who moved from friend to therapist with remarkable agility), and living proof that miracles do happen.

"There are only two ways to live life," wrote Albert Einstein. "One is as though nothing were a miracle. The other is as though everything were a miracle."

In my depressed state, I was inclined to the former. Now, I lean toward the latter.

Thanks, Harold.

*The wonderful thing about saints
is that they were human.
They lost their tempers,
scolded God,
were egotistical or testy
or impatient in their turns,
made mistakes and regretted them.
Still they went on doggedly
blundering toward heaven.*

PHYLLIS MCGINLEY

INDEX

*The real voyage of discovery
consists not in
seeking new landscapes
but in having new eyes.*

MARCEL PROUST

Of further interest

You Can Feel Good Again
Richard Carlson

Many cures for depression have been proposed over the years. Nearly all of them have said it is necessary to explore in depth the sufferer's feelings and past trauma. And most of them have failed. Now a radical new approach suggests a much simpler solution, one that is within everyone's grasp without the need for professional help. You can feel good again if you grasp that:

- your thoughts determine the way you feel
- thinking about problems only makes them worse
- analysing negative thoughts and feelings is the worst thing you can do
- thinking is not something that happens to you, but something you do to create your experience
- thoughts you produce when you're unhappy are inevitably negative and therefore not to be trusted
- thoughts come and go – you're free to choose at any moment which you hold on to and which you let go of
- you can learn to dismiss negative thoughts and find inner contentment

Recommended by doctors and therapists, including Waynne Dyer and Gerald Jampolsky, Richard Carlson's simple yet direct approach offers a realistic route away from depression – towards happiness.

You Can't Afford the Luxury of a Negative Thought

John-Roger and Peter McWilliams

It is one of the most serious diseases of our time, obstructing us from believing that we really *deserve* happiness: an attitude which affects us mentally, physically and emotionally. Negative thinking can provide the right environment for illness to prosper. How important it is, then, for those with serious illnesses *not* to indulge in it.

The cure is simple. *Savour* the positive in your life; weed out the negative; *enjoy* each moment. The path is not easy but this best-selling book will infect you with its sense of fun and its gregarious wisdom. Packed with inspirational quotes, it will unlock new possibilities in your life as well as being both compelling and uplifting reading. Accept *your* right to live life to the full!

'A work of unique simplicity which offers a way of thinking and living in which motives are high but realistic and available. I love it.' — Pauline Collins

| YOU CAN FEEL GOOD AGAIN | 0 7225 2867 1 | £5.99 | ☐ |

YOU CAN'T AFFORD THE LUXURY
  OF A NEGATIVE THOUGHT   0 7225 2383 1 £9.99 ☐

WEALTH 101   0 7225 2855 8 £9.99 ☐

All these books are available from your local bookseller or can be ordered direct from the publishers.

To order direct just tick the titles you want and fill in the form below:

Name: _____

Address: _____

_____

_____ Postcode: _____

Send to Thorsons Mail Order, Dept 3, HarperCollins*Publishers*, Westerhill Road, Bishopbriggs, Glasgow G64 2QT.
Please enclose a cheque or postal order or your authority to debit your Visa/Access account –

Credit card no: _____

Expiry date: _____

Signature: _____

– to the value of the cover price plus:
UK & BFPO: Add £1.00 for the first book and 25p for each additional book ordered.
Overseas orders including Eire: please add £2.95 service charge. Books will be sent by surface mail but quotes for airmail despatches will be given on request.

24-HOUR TELEPHONE ORDERING SERVICE FOR ACCESS/VISA CARDHOLDERS - TEL: 0141 772 2281.